PRESERVING LONDON

PRESERVING LONDON

KATHLEEN DENBIGH

*With 58 Drawings and 26 Maps
by the Author*

ROBERT HALE · LONDON

ISBN 0 7091 6732 6

Robert Hale Limited
Clerkenwell House
Clerkenwell Green
London EC1

Photoset in Great Britain by
Specialised Offset Services Limited, Liverpool
and printed by
REDWOOD BURN LIMITED
Trowbridge & Esher

Contents

To Marilyn and Sally
and the young generation

Acknowledgements

My thanks are due to the Southwark Library Services for permission to base the drawings of Dulwich Village on those contained in the *Story of Dulwich*; similarly to Mr G.A. Renvoize in respect of the drawing of the Church of St Mary, Merton; and to the Vicar and Churchwardens of the Church of St Anne, Kew.

K.D.

Illustrations

Preface

This book is not about national monuments or famous buildings, most of which have long since been protected by preservation orders. (If these are mentioned, as in the section on Greenwich, it is simply because they are part of the overall scene.) Nor is it about the traditional tourist haunts of central London* whose merits are already well known.

It is a book about the *conservation areas* of Greater London – areas designated in recent years as worthy of protection and possible improvement because of their special qualities and the contribution they make to the whole environment.

Many of these places are still little known and, although the ones I have chosen to write about include some of the giants such as Blackheath and Highgate, they also include the 'pocket handkerchiefs' such as Pinner High Street and Kingston Old Town. In fact all types and shapes and sizes of conservation area are represented, with a geographical spread as far north as Forty Hill in the London Borough of Enfield and as far south as Carshalton in the London Borough of Sutton.

The common factor is that all have something unique to offer in terms of character, beauty, charm or interest and that collectively they add a whole extra dimension to the heritage of a great capital city.

K.D.

* The Appendix contains a complete list of the Conservation Areas of Greater London, including those of central London.

Enfield

Barnet

Harrow

Haringey

Waltham
Forest

Redbridge

Brent

Camden

Islington

Hackney

Havering

Hillingdon

Ealing

Kensington & Chelsea

City of Westminster

City

Tower Hamlets

Newham

Barking

Hammersmith

Hounslow

Rich-mond up on Thames

Wandsworth

Lambeth

Southwark

Greenwich

River Thames

Bexley

Kingston-upon-Thames

Merton

Lewisham

Sutton

Croydon

Bromley

10 Miles

Introduction

A growing awareness of the modern threat to historic towns, villages and village suburbs helped to pave the way for the Civic Amenities Act of 1967 and the 'conservation area' which it created.

Under the terms of the Act, local authorities were encouraged to designate any area of architectural or historic interest within their boroughs which they considered worthy of protection and improvement. The idea was not to produce museums or collections of monuments, but to help places of special merit to keep their character and individuality while continuing to play an active part in the life of the community.

No Act of Parliament could have been more overdue. Although the Town and Country Planning Acts of 1944 and 1947 had vastly extended the statutory listing system for buildings of historic merit, the building boom of the 1950s and 1960s produced, in the name of progress, a spate of demolitions on a scale never before experienced. Even listed buildings fell daily to the bulldozer while other buildings which collectively made an important visual or aesthetic contribution to their surroundings received even less quarter. Nobody seemed to know how to stop these irreparable losses and even that resilient group of people, the conservationists, were beginning to experience a sense of hopelessness.

The casualties included many old high streets, some of which were transformed almost overnight from ancient market places into faceless shopping centres of supermarkets and chain stores. Far too often the new owners showed little or no concern for the fate of the original buildings previously occupied by small shops, nor for the effect which their new plastic frontages were likely to have upon the overall scene. No less insidious was the disappearance of dwelling houses of character to make way for more blocks of flats and the gradual shrinkage of open spaces.

These vanishing acts were in full flood at the time that Mr Duncan Sandys founded the Civic Trust in 1957. The Trust was formed with some clearly defined objectives, namely to encourage high quality in architecture, to preserve buildings of distinction and historic interest, to protect the beauties of the countryside, to eliminate and prevent ugliness whether from bad design or neglect, to stimulate interest in the good appearance of town and country, and to inspire generally a sense of civic pride. It was these objectives and the Civic Trust's gallant efforts to take a practical lead in all matters concerning the environment that finally led to the passing of the Civic Amenities Act ten years later, in 1967.

The new Act was different from its predecessors in that it was concerned with places rather than with individual buildings and that it introduced the idea of architectural group value. Local authorities were directed to determine areas of special architectural or historic interest in their towns and boroughs and to do their best to preserve and enhance their character by according them special treatment.

The Civic Amenities Act was a valuable declaration of interest in the environment but from the practical standpoint it had few real teeth. To begin with there was very little money available to support its recommendations and too much depended upon the enthusiasm or ability of each individual town or borough to take advantage of the new provisions. In fact such were the limitations and problems associated with these provisions that some local authorities scarcely responded at all.

In addition to the practical deterrents, conservation was still far from being a popular cause and it was all too common for private owners, developers, builders and antipathetic town or borough councillors to set themselves up as realists trying to meet modern demands in the face of opposition. The opposing forces were variously accused of trying to uphold the old order, of burying their heads in the past or ignoring the human needs of other people. Armed with such arguments, many a council, including the Greater London Council, sanctioned demolitions only to concede at later dates that the buildings they pulled down, or wanted to pull down, made an important contribution to the amenity and character of the areas concerned.

By the beginning of the 1970s it was realised that, if the Civic Amenities Act was to be really effective, further legislation was needed and the Town and Country Planning Act (1971) and the Town and Country Planning (Amendment) Act (1972) were passed.

Under the new consolidating legislation, local authorities found themselves with extended powers – powers to specify buildings within their conservation areas which could not be demolished without permission, whether or not those buildings were on the statutory list. Finally, in 1974, the Town and Country Amenities Act made it an offence for an owner to demolish *any* building in a conservation area without first obtaining a demolition order and a planning permit for redevelopment.

This more positive control has done much to strengthen the position of the conservation area but whether or not it goes far enough to prevent harmful planning applications from succeeding in the future remains to be seen. There are still some towns and boroughs where proposals for unsuitable redevelopment get through in the end simply because they do not go too far in density and in height. Perhaps the only reliable maxim for a conservation area should be: No change without improvement.

Unfortunately there have also been plenty of cases where only small penalties have been imposed for actual flouting of the law. According to the *Architects' Journal*, one listed building is still being lost every day, partly because there are no sanctions against neglectful owners who allow their properties to decay to the point where they have to be pulled down for safety reasons.

Nor are these the only problems facing conservation areas. There is still the obtrusive effect of peripheral buildings such as tower blocks which, although sited outside the designated territory, continue to appear and cast their shadows over whole areas.

There is also the bogey of excessive traffic. Far too many historic town centres are still being shaken to their foundations and too many old village suburbs turned into circuses simply because the motorist is given precedence over the pedestrian or because nobody has succeeded in devising an effective system of control. In all these matters perhaps the best hope of finding a solution lies in winning the interest, co-operation and support of the general public.

Fortunately the growth of the 'amenity lobby' is accelerating. Both nationally and locally, civic societies, conservation societies, preservation societies and environment groups, all with similar if not identical aims, are either springing up or increasing their membership as more people begin to understand what conservation is about and that it is likely to affect the quality both of their own and of their children's lives. There are now well over a thousand such groups linked to the Civic Trust alone – an organisation whose purpose, among other things, is to advise and help all local amenity groups without necessarily being committed to their policies and actions. In their turn, the affiliated societies, especially those concerned with conservation areas, are being consulted and listened to by the planning departments of local authorities.

By the end of 1975 there were well over three thousand designated conservation areas in the country as a whole, of which about a tenth belong to the thirty-two boroughs over which the Greater London Council became overlord in 1965. As elsewhere, some of the London boroughs were quicker off the mark in designating suitable territories than were others. Some produced long lists while others displayed little or no enthusiasm. However in this connection it has to be remembered that natural endowment is often a major determining factor. Richmond-upon-Thames, for example, has an impressive list of nineteen conservation areas, but this is a borough rich in history where royal palaces once abounded and where the River Thames continues to provide a setting of natural beauty even for its most urbanised of village suburbs. Far less fortunate are those London boroughs, particularly to the east, where history appears to have passed by or where most of its traces have been obliterated.

But conservation areas have no walls around them. They are open all day and everyday without charge to all who wish to enjoy their unique qualities and most of them can be reached by public transport. To me, every one has something special to offer and is worth writing about. In fact it was a matter of considerable regret when I realised that to include all those in Greater London was an impossible task and that some selection for a single book would have to be made. I did however decide to aim at a fairly wide geographical spread and to include examples of all types of conservation area.

It is for this reason that the reader will find no fixed criterion: some of those included are very small, others quite extensive; some have a wealth of listed buildings, others hardly any; some depend upon a quality of magnificence, others on simple environmental features such as old village greens, market places and mature landscapes. The choice was never easy, though I did make a point of including most of those classified by the G.L.C. Historic Buildings Board as 'outstanding', and I also pandered to some extent to my own convenience and personal fancies.

My hope is that this visual and historical exploration of twenty-five conservation areas around London will help people to appreciate and enjoy places which are part of their heritage and will also encourage them to visit other areas of equal interest and merit within their reach. A full list of designated areas within the various London boroughs is given in the Appendix.

For those to whom all these places are inaccessible, my hope is that the visual gap will be filled, at least in part, by the maps and illustrations.

1

Blackheath

Shops and drinking fountain

The charm and special character of Blackheath may appear elusive at first sight because of the great traffic vortex which not only preoccupies those who wish to stay alive but also seems to suck one in from almost every point towards the concentrated chaos at the centre.

However it is the centre which provides the vital clue to an understanding of Blackheath because it was here, at the lower end of Tranquil Vale not far from where Blackheath Station now stands at the bottom of the hill, that development first began towards the end of the eighteenth century. Until then the village was virtually non-existent and only the junction of several small cross routes foreshadowed the shape of things to come.

By 1820 two more roads, this time radiating outwards to link the vale with the historic heath at the top, had been formed, both with buildings on them. Tranquil Vale, the picturesque but busy shopping street which still clings to its original and now wholly inappropriate name, was one of them

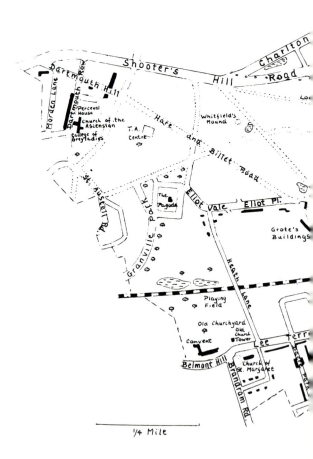

¼ Mile

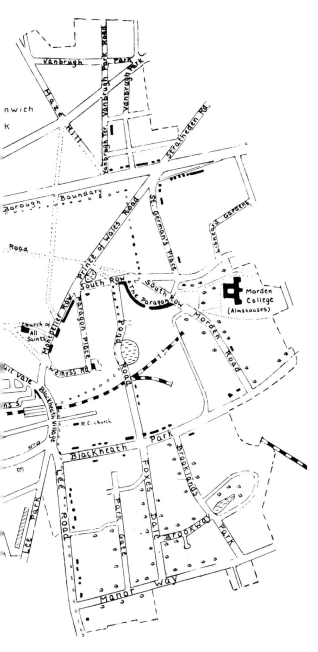

and its more easterly neighbour, Montpelier, was the other.

These two roads, meeting at a V-shaped junction at the bottom of the hill, clearly helped to lay the foundations of the intractable modern problem, though it was the arrival of the North Kent Railway in 1849 and subsequent surge in population that set the final seal on it.

Yet, as one soon begins to realise, the old rural atmosphere has survived and, even in those parts of the conservation territory where fine old Georgian and Regency houses have become heavily diluted with modern development, its subtle presence continues to preserve a sense of village identity.

The existence of two designated conservation areas instead of a single one is simply accounted for by the current borough boundary which runs roughly north and south down through the middle of this expansive area. The area which includes most of the heath and the land to the west of Lee Road, belongs to the London Borough of Lewisham whereas the territory to the east, elongated northward to include the Vanbrugh estate, belongs to the London Borough of Greenwich. However to the historian or explorer such artificial divisions mean nothing.

Historically it was the heath, that windswept plateau of grass and scrub on its natural escarpment with extensive views over Kent and Surrey that was important. It was the gateway to London from the south-east and here it was, along the line of the modern Shooter's Way that the Romans built a branch of Watling Street – a vital road between the capital and the Straits of Dover and one which was later to become famous as the romantic highway of pilgrims, statesmen, highwaymen and kings.

For centuries this road and the wide open space that surrounded it seems to have attracted one rebellious army after another, not one of them successful. Among those who camped here was Wat Tyler protesting against excessive taxes at the time of the Peasants' Revolt in 1381, Jack Cade who led the uprising of 1450, Lord Audley and the Cornish rebels whose slaughtered remains in 1497 were buried under various mounds, notably Whitfield's Mound, and finally Thomas Wyatt who unsuccessfully led the men of Kent against Mary I in 1554.

But in addition to being a scene of lost causes, the heath has seen plenty of pageant in its time. Henry V was greeted here by the Lord Mayor of London on his victorious return from

Agincourt and a century later, in 1540, Anne of Cleaves was received here with extravagant ceremony by her unwieldy royal suitor, Henry VIII.

Yet for all its historic and glamorous moments the heath, whose thick black looking gorse provided almost unlimited cover, was regarded as a very dangerous place for travellers and it was not until after the accidental destruction of the gorse which had been set on fire to amuse George IV's wife, Queen Caroline, that the scene began to change. A few houses already existed around the periphery, but now that the gorse had gone and there was the added protection of a newly formed police force (1829), a building spree began to get under way similar to one which had already started lower down the hill at what is now regarded as the centre of Blackheath.

If one decides to start from the centre by walking up Tranquil Vale from the railway station, it is easy to see how the earlier development began. The oldest group of buildings in sight are those on the left-hand side opposite the V-shaped junction (blissfully provided with a pedestrian crossing) with Montpelier. The ground floors of this group, Nos 23 to 25 Tranquil Vale, were all converted in the nineteenth century to form shop fronts but the buildings themselves date back to the middle of the previous century and are considered typical of that period. A little higher up the street, the tiny cul-de-sac called Collins Square, with its two clapboard cottages, is probably older still, marking the spot where people lived before the village developed.

Although Tranquil Vale veers round to the west, beyond the shops and drinking fountain, as the Heath comes into sight near the top of the hill, one can scarcely fail to notice All Saints' Church standing in solitary isolation on its easterly plot of open heathland. Conspicuous and therefore an important feature of the Blackheath conservation area, this small Gothic-style church with the broach spire, described by Pevsner as looking like a model, was built in 1857-67 by the architect Benjamin Ferrey.

Closer at hand, at the corner of the crescent on the left of Tranquil Vale, the grey-coloured house with the ornamental pierced parapet and two-storeyed projecting bow window has long been known as Eastnor House. Attractively but economically conserved, both this house, No 1 Lloyds Place, and its two immediate neighbours were built in the late

eighteenth century – a little earlier than No 4 which appeared
in 1800.

Farther back from the road, the prominent and beautifully
co-ordinated group of brick houses of various heights and sizes
known as Grotes Buildings belongs to the middle of the
eighteenth century, while the picturesque pair on the
remaining side of the crescent, Nos 1 and 2 Grotes Place, are
of early nineteenth-century vintage. With the heath and pond
for foreground, these last two are believed to be among the
most photographed houses in Blackheath.

The row which comes into sight as one rounds the next
corner into Eliot Place was also built in the late eighteenth
and early nineteenth century. Sir James Clark-Ross (1800-
62), the polar explorer, lived in the tall narrow house, No 2,
next to the detached and more impressive Heathfield House
with its recent side extension to form a block of flats.

The only houses in the continuation road, Eliot Vale, which
belong to the old era are Nos 8 and 9. Both have been
extensively altered and, in one case, neglected, but the
charming group, Nos 3, 4 and 5 The Meadway, tucked
peacefully away in the adjacent cul-de-sac, are unmistakably
Georgian.

Apart from Pagoda House, which now stands in the new
road called Pagoda Gardens leading down from the top of
Eliot Vale to the landscaped council flats in the hollow, this
completes the important cluster of eighteenth-century
architecture at the southern edge of the heath. Shaped like a
pagoda and the only one of its kind in Blackheath, Pagoda
House was built as a garden house by the fourth Earl of
Cardigan in the third part of the eighteenth century and was
later enlarged. In recent years it was acquired by the local
authority and there has been much debate over its future.

The boundary of the conservation area follows roughly the
route around the heath which leads to that other important
cluster of listed properties at the north-west corner. It cuts
across Granville Park to Eliot Hill and then follows the path
called St Austell Road to Lewisham Hill, Dartmouth Row
and Morden Lane.

Dartmouth Row, with its impressive collection of old
properties, was named after Lord Dartmouth, principal
adviser to James II. It was he who, as Admiral Legge, bought
the Blackheath estate and later, in 1683, obtained the charter
for a fair – the fair which has been held on the heath at certain

The Pagoda

times of the year ever since and is now held on the large triangle of land on the north side of Shooter's Hill Road.

Although there is obviously good reason to remember this seventeenth-century lord of the manor, it is worth remembering that there were other well documented ownerships long before his time. In Anglo-Saxon times Blackheath was part of the estate given by King Alfred to his youngest daughter Elstrudis, probably as a marriage portion. When eventually Elstrudis handed it over to the abbey at Ghent as a memorial to her husband it became known as the land of St Peter of Ghent and remained so until seized in 1414 by Henry V who gave it to the Carthusian priory at Sheen in Surrey as part of an endowment. Although several changes of ownership occurred after the dissolution of the monasteries, stability returned with the purchase by Lord Dartmouth, whose heirs continued as lords of the manor almost up to the present century.

The large eighteenth-century brick building at the southern corner of Dartmouth Row, now mainly used for conferences, was formerly Dartmouth House and was owned by the Dartmouth family until they sold it to the College of Greyladies towards the end of the last century. The 'grey ladies' were trained church workers who wore a sort of grey uniform and operated from the Church of the Ascension a few yards higher up.

The Church of the Ascension was founded between 1690 and 1695 as a proprietary church by a lady called Mrs Susannah Graham and was originally known as the Blackheath Chapel. The nave dates from about 1834 but the apse, with its plaster semi-dome, is part of the original building.

In Pevsner's view, the long two-storeyed red brick building with the stone quoins which stands well back from the road and is now known as Perceval House and Spencer House, Nos 21 and 23 Dartmouth Row, is 'uncommonly good'. It was built between 1690 and 1700 and became the home, in 1812, of Spencer Perceval who achieved posthumous fame that same year by being assassinated in the lobby of the House of Commons by a bankrupt Liverpool broker.

The attractive row of houses a little further up on the opposite (west) side of Dartmouth Row, Nos 36a to 28, were built in the early to mid-eighteenth century while Nos 22 and 20, just short of the corner shop, date back to about 1700. Until it was pulled down about 1906 to make way for the present villas, an old house of similar date stood between these two groups.

The three-storeyed house of painted brick with the Greek Doric wood porch just round the corner in Dartmouth Hill was also built in the mid-eighteenth century. Although known as Montague House, it has no connection with the great house of the same name which until 1815 stood at the south-west corner of Greenwich Park and was once leased by the Prince Regent's estranged wife, Queen Caroline. Nearer the heath, the two houses with the little railed-in courtyard, Nos 22 and 20 Dartmouth Hill, began life as a single late eighteenth-century residence which was later occupied by James Glaisher (1809-1903), astronomer, meteorologist and pioneer of weather forecasting.

The house called Sherwell at the end of Dartmouth Hill and the one called Lydia at the end of Dartmouth Grove, which together form a stone-fronted pair facing directly on to Wat Tyler Road and the heath, also made their appearance in the late eighteenth century as part of the encircling process.

After crossing Wat Tyler Road (named after the unfortunate rebel who once camped here), one can take the Hare and Billet Road across the open stretches of turfed land that leads back to Tranquil Vale.

The heath is still one of south-east London's major open spaces and it is interesting to recall that this was where golf was first played in England. Shortly after his arrival from Scotland, James I introduced the game and the Royal Blackheath Golf Club was founded in 1608.

With the solitary church of All Saints as a guiding landmark, one is soon back at the small pond near Grotes Place. This and the various other ponds scattered around Blackheath, including the centrally situated one in Pond Road, were originally formed out of pits for the excavation of

The Paragon

gravel. Retained in their natural settings, they now make their own contributions to the conservation areas.

Running north and south only a short distance beyond the church and Montpelier Row, Pond Road forms part of the Lewisham–Greenwich borough boundary. The result is that Montpelier Row, with its important late eighteenth-century three and four-storeyed houses, Nos 12 to 16, and South Row with its Colonnade House, built about 1795, are in Lewisham territory whereas both Paragon House and the pond on the east side of the street belong to the London Borough of Greenwich.

Among the latter's most highly prized possessions is The Paragon itself. With its paired houses linked by white colonnades, the famous crescent is now rated as one of the finest architectural groups in London. It was severely damaged during the last war but has since been very successfully restored without loss of character and converted into self-contained flats suitable for modern living. It probably looks little different now from what it did when first built about 1790 to the design of the architect Michael Searles.

The conservation area includes the tongue of land to the north of The Paragon beyond Shooter's Hill Road and east of Greenwich Park where the name 'Vanbrugh' occurs on many of the streets. Sir John Vanbrugh was the architect who designed Blenheim Palace and who, in 1719, built himself the great brick pile with medieval turrets (now Vanbrugh Castle School) which stands lower down the hill in the adjacent Greenwich Village conservation area.

Back on the south side of Shooter's Hill Road, the boundary of the Blackheath conservation area follows the line of Liskeard Gardens and part of Kidbrooke Grove, thereby taking in the whole of Morden College.

This beautifully kept establishment just east of The Paragon was founded by Sir John Morden in 1695 for 'poor merchants' whose future had been ruined by "perils of the sea or other unavoidable accidents". It is still in use as a charitable institution and is not normally open to the public but the glimpse one gets from Kidbrooke Gardens of the red brick building with its attractive clock front speaks for itself. Constructed around a large cloistered quadrangle, the main building was for many years attributed to Wren but it is now generally believed to have been the work of Sir Edward Strong, contractor for the Greenwich Seamen's Hospital.

Nowadays each resident member of the college has his own apartment, with domestic help provided as well as a pension allowance of up to £200 per annum.

Several of the houses in Morden Road, the road that links The Paragon with the network of delightful tree-lined roads in the south-eastern part of the conservation area, date back to the Regency period. Over the years some have had distinguished residents, including the composer Charles Gounod (1818-93) who in 1870 stayed at No 15.

However, the finest of these roads must surely be Blackheath Park, now mercifully provided with road ramps to slow down the traffic. Many of the earlier houses here are superb examples of the Georgian and Regency periods, built well before the appearance of St Michael's Church in their midst at the corner with Pond Road.

St Michael's has been described as an extravagant example of the Gothic Revival period. With its grey brick exterior and its series of internal roof timbers shaped like the Bridge of Sighs in Venice, it was designed by George Smith and built in 1829 as a proprietary chapel for the developing Blackheath estate. It is particularly noted for its delicate pinnacled spire sometimes known as 'the Needle of Kent'.

Because they have blended in so well with the semi-rural atmosphere, some of the newer roads such as Brooklands Park and Foxes Dale have been included in the Blackheath conservation area, with Manor Way serving as the southern boundary east of Lee Road.

Lee Road forms part of the boundary between the two boroughs, taking one back past the small but interesting group of bow-fronted mid-eighteenth-century houses, Nos 6 to 14 even, to the busy main street called Blackheath Village which merges into Tranquil Vale just beyond the railway station.

All that now remains of the conservation area lies westward along the length of Lee Terrace south of the railway line. It takes in the pocket of old terraces on the south side of the road and comes to an end at the church of St Margaret on the corner with Brandram Road.

This final and conspicuous landmark, with its solid picturesque west tower, was built as a 'new' church by J. Brown in 1839-41 to replace a medieval one dating back to the fifteenth century. The old church stood on the opposite side of the road where large eighteenth- and nineteenth-century monuments still stand with a curious small ruin in their midst. Clearly visible from the road, the ruin is a relic of the old church tower. Its front acquired the concrete rendering during the nineteenth century, presumably with the hope of preserving or embellishing it.

Along with Blackheath's open spaces, trees, ponds and carefully integrated newer developments, such oddities are now recognised as valuable assets worthy of conservation, but they do not alter the basic character of this outstanding village suburb. That clearly remains firmly rooted in the 'age of elegance' which endowed it with so much fine domestic architecture.

2

Carshalton Village

The Ponds and church of All Saints

Standing in the leafy shades of Honeywood Walk beside Carshalton's two famous central ponds, it is hard to believe that this old village, situated at the foot of the Surrey hills some three miles from Croydon, is now a suburb of Greater London. Perhaps the only way to really convince oneself is by diverting one's eyes across the expanse of water to the red double-decker buses ploughing their way around the periphery, along North Street and Pound Street.

Until this century Carshalton, at the head of the River Wandle, was in fact almost untouched by the outside world. Its old houses and cottages, many of which still survive, were well supplied with water by the great network of underground springs which fed the ponds, while their inhabitants could still find work on the old manor farms.

That world vanished yet parts of the old village, including the ponds, survived, thereby bequeathing to this co-opted territory of south London the delightful Carshalton village conservation area.

So important were the ponds to every conservationist that one can imagine the alarm and despondency when it was discovered earlier this century that some of the springs which fed them were drying up. Something had to be done and it was for this reason that in 1972, as part of an environmental improvement scheme, they were lined with concrete and given an additional water supply. Now all is well again – as was proved during the heavy autumn and winter rains of 1974 when reputedly every pool and stream in Carshalton came gushing back to life with such vigour that flocks of gulls arrived on the scene to join the resident swans and refused to depart.

No doubt it was just such a scene in 1653 when the diarist

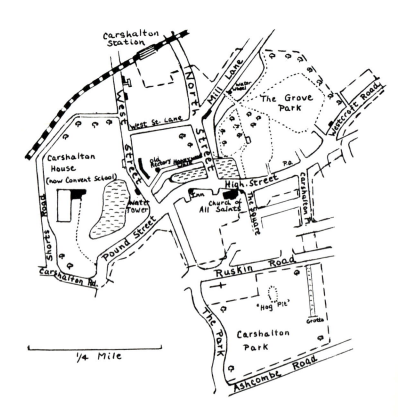

John Evelyn visited the village and reported it as being "excellently watered". In those days Carshalton was noted for its trout, its lucrative walnut and cherry trees, and for its water-cress and brewing.

As one might guess, Carshalton's good water supply was a key factor in its early history and the discovery of Neolithic and Bronze Age relics in and around the parish evoked no real surprise. The Saxons also appear to have recognised its merits and probably built the first church – on the site of the present one which is Norman in origin.

Perched on its high bank at the corner of the main road overlooking the ponds, the church of All Saints (open daily from 10 a.m. to noon) provides some important clues to Carshalton's later history. Most of the building consists of a nineteenth-century enlargement but the small protruding section on the east (left-hand facing) side dates back to the twelfth century. This is the Lady Chapel which formed the chancel of the original church and which is now notable for its colourfully inscribed marble altar tomb installed by Nicholas Gaynesford, lord of Carshalton's sub-manor, before he died in 1498.

The huge monuments facing each other from the two ends of the outer south aisle depict two later Carshalton worthies who also left their mark on the old village. Since both in their time tried to establish their social supremacy, it is interesting to note the final result! The white marble monument which grandiosely portrays a gentleman in recumbent posture propped up on his left elbow and resting his right arm on a laurel-wreathed skull is that of Sir William Scawen, a one-time governor of the Bank of England who, in 1696, bought an important part of the divided Carshalton manor east of the ponds, whereas the competing tall Georgian monument at the opposite (west) end of the aisle is that of Sir John Fellowes. Sir John Fellowes was also a financier and in 1714 he became owner of the extensive Carshalton House estate on the west side – an estate which today is still almost intact and forms a substantial part of the conservation area.

If one sets out from the church via Pound Street for this hillside estate, it is interesting to reflect on route on the merits of the modern intrusion which appeared in 1967. Although the award-winning development of sheltered housing for the elderly, which now occupies much of the street's frontage overlooking the ponds, was specifically designed to make it blend in with the old, there was considerable initial misgiving. Not only did the project mean the demolition of old property but that which was left, notably the two early nineteenth-century cottages at the top of the steep Church Hill cul-de-sac adjacent to the church, became partially obscured. However, after some favourable comment in the architectural press, the new development now appears to be an accepted part of the landscape.

Perhaps it was partly as a conciliatory gesture to the historically-minded that the architects of this project and the sculptor associated with it finally presented the tall colourful statue of Anne Boleyn which stands so prominently in the corner niche – despite the fact that there appears to be little or no evidence to support the popular tradition that this luckless lady once rode through the village and that a well "burst forth from a stroke of her horse's hoof". As the cynics continue to point out, the small circular plot of land near by, now enclosed by railings and embellished with a bush and a Gothic-lettered inscription proclaiming it to be the 'Boleyn Well', most likely got its name through the Norman lord of the manor (from Boulogne?) rather than from Henry VIII's second wife.

The part weather-boarded Greyhound Inn which still stands opposite the south-west corner of the ponds is believed to date back to about 1700, while the Orchard Hill cul-de-sac just beyond is part of an ancient pathway. As one might guess, Pound Street itself takes its name from the pound for stray animals which once stood close by.

The high red brick enclosing wall which flanks West Street and the hilly end of Pound Street heralds the beginning of the Carshalton House estate. In 1893 both land and house were acquired by the Daughters of the Cross and are now occupied by St Philomena's Roman Catholic School for Girls. There is no exact information about the origin of the site but when the present driveway was being constructed a great quantity of human bones were discovered, suggesting that it may once have been a Saxon battlefield.

The fine seventeenth-century mansion which eventually took the place of an earlier house and still stands was built in 1696 by a tobacco merchant called Edward Carleton. Excluding the school extensions, it then had, and still has, the equivalent of seven bedrooms on each of its two upper floors and a number of 'parlours' on the ground floor.

Unfortunately for Edward Carleton, his occupation was

short-lived. In 1713 he was in debt to the tune of £16,000 for customs duties and the house and grounds were advertised for sale in the *London Gazette*. They were bought the following year by Sir John Radcliffe, the Oxford benefactor who was physician to Queen Anne and who is said to have been so disturbed by her death that he too died shortly afterwards in the same year. This time when the property came up for sale it was bought by Thomas Scawen, son of Sir William, who sold it a year later to Sir John Fellowes.

Although not immune from misfortune – as sub-governor of the ill-fated South Sea Company, he had to spend a brief spell in the Tower when the 'bubble' burst – Sir John Fellowes appears to have had more staying power than his predecessors and not only succeeded in completing many striking additions to the estate but also managed to die a rich man in 1724. Both the initial 'F' inscribed in the form of a crest in the wrought iron entrance gates and the stone lion crest on the pillars are his. He was responsible for the landscape gardening, the sweep of the drive where the house comes suddenly into view, the form of the ornamental lake and the construction of the large lakeside grotto known as 'The Hermitage'. He also built the colonnade to the west of the house and, last but not least, the huge red brick water tower which backs so prominently on to West Street.

Although perhaps not very unusual in John Fellowes' day, the water tower, or waterhouse as it is sometimes called, is now regarded as a near-unique specimen of its kind. The tower held a huge lead-lined reservoir which was kept full by pumping water up to it from a lakeside spring by power generated from the outfall of the lake. This ingenious and economical arrangement ensured a copious supply of water to every part of both mansion and stables and appears never to have failed. And, just as the estate's natural resources were fully utilised, so was the space beneath the tower. In addition to the machinery, the ground floor contained an orangery, a 'saloon', a bathroom and a dressing-room – all of them now transformed and usefully employed as classrooms!

The conservation area stretches northward up West Street past the back of the water tower as far as the railway line. The tiny detached cottage, No 2 West Street, was built about 1700 and its neighbours, which form part of the white weather-boarded row numbered 6 to 10A, also date back to the early eighteenth century. Much of the property in this street originated about 1800, including the very new looking white painted terrace which is a drastically restored group of old cottages. The larger weather-boarded house, No 70 West Street, near the railway bridge, belongs to the eighteenth century.

If one turns eastward along Festival Walk in the direction of the ponds, it is pleasant to guess at the height of the huge plane tree which still stands at the far end, on the bank of the stream. According to the *Guinness Book of Records*, it is 125 feet high and the tallest in Britain.

The Old Rectory

In recent years the typical square Queen Anne house on the north side of the path, now used as offices for local government and voluntary organisations but still known as the Old Rectory, was purchased by the council as part of a far-sighted policy of preservation. In fact most of the area north of Festival Walk and its delightful continuation path, Honeywood Walk, with its open view of the church across the ponds, is now the home of council offices.

So too is the large public park called The Grove whose enclosing red brick wall on the eastern side of North Street can already be seen. The house known as Stone Court which stands just inside the larger of North Street's two entrance gates and is at present used by the Department of Education is the thrice rebuilt manor house of the old sub-manor of Carshalton.

Stone Court was once the domain of Nicholas Gaynesford, fifteenth-century lord of the sub-manor, whose colourful altar tomb stands in the church. Nicholas Gaynesford was a man unusually adept at switching his allegiance from one monarch to another and, despite a period in the Tower of London under Richard III, he managed to live through five reigns, from Henry VI to Henry VII. It was not until its latter years that Stone Court may have become the miller's house – a theory arising partly from the presence of the big water-wheel that still stands beside the sluggish pool and nearby foot-bridge. The roof and cage over the wheel are of course modern, erected to try to protect the rusty paddles from further disintegration.

The main stream which crosses this very pleasant park in a north-easterly direction leads eventually to the River Wandle. The single eyesore and blotch on the horizon, namely the huge and increasing piles of metal drums over to the north-west, belong to an expanding chemical works. Needless to say, they are eyed by Carshalton's conservationists with disfavour and some apprehension.

One can leave the park via Westcroft Road where a house (now council offices) of sixteenth-century origin still survives. Alternatively one can emerge into the equally busy High Street beside the modern post office nearly opposite Carshalton Place on the south side of the street, with its open canal in the middle.

The conservation area does not include the built-up area immediately to the west of Carshalton Place where 'Mascalls', the manor house of Thomas Scawen once stood, but it does include, as a separate unit, Carshalton Park at the far side of Ruskin Road which was once part of the 'Mascalls' estate.

Although it has long aroused much interest and speculation, the origin of the large sunken dell just inside the park's Ruskin Road entrance remains something of a mystery. One theory put forward to explain this unnatural looking formation known locally as the 'hogpit' is that it is an old chalk pit grown over with grass. Whatever it is or was, it is now very popular with the children, especially on the rare occasions when it turns itself into a lake, as it did in 1974-5.

Carshalton Park's other special point of interest is the old grotto near its southern boundary close to where the canal disappears underground. This was created by Thomas Scawen, perhaps in emulation of 'The Hermitage' built by John Fellowes on the neighbouring Carshalton House estate.

If one returns to the traffic congested High Street via The Square, it is still possible to think back several centuries. The tiny white-washed dwelling, No 6 High Street, now a butcher's shop at the corner beside the church, is believed to be the oldest house in Carshalton and was probably the home of the Priest. Its timber framing is said to date back to the fifteenth-century.

As part of the old manor wall, the small area of chequer-work masonry incorporated into the churchyard wall behind this tiny dwelling is probably almost as old and there are hopes that eventually it will be restored. However, as the Carshalton Society points out, until there is a by-pass to relieve Carshalton village of its heavy traffic, lorries and double-decker buses will continue to wear away *all* its old walls, and restorative work will continue to outstrip available funds.

But having accepted the fact that there is still plenty of rescue work to be done – quite apart from that of extricating motorists who still regularly and unintentionally take a dip in its famous ponds on dark nights! – one can hardly fail but admire the way this ancient village-turned-suburb still preserves its identity.

3

Dulwich Village

Georgian houses in College Road

Green verges, overhanging trees, elegant Georgian houses, a famous school and an important picture gallery only five miles south-east of central London sound like riches enough for any conservation area, yet here in Dulwich Village there is something more; there is also that intangible quality possessed by places stamped with a human personality.

Dulwich was once the domain of Edward Alleyn, the actor son of a Bishopsgate inn-keeper, who achieved fame on the Elizabethan stage and chose, as part of the fruits of his success, to establish himself in the tiny hamlet as lord of the manor. His benefactions were modest, yet in one form or another most of them survived and today, nearly four centuries later, the original Dulwich College still controls much of the land.

Even if one starts at the busy junction where the small modern shops stand near the northern end of the main street (now called Dulwich Village but formerly, until about 1912, known as the High Street), one's eye is immediately drawn to the old burial ground which the Elizabethan benefactor gave to the hamlet in 1616.

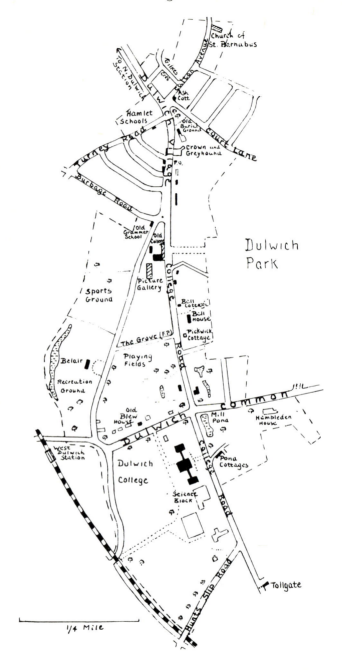

Needless to say, the old cemetery's continued occupation of the V-shaped junction between the two main roads has attracted the attention not only of admirers but of would-be road wideners throughout most of the present century and it is still something of a wonder that it remains intact. The last person to be buried in its leafy grounds was Betsy Goodman whose father and grandfather had both been landlords of the old Crown Inn. Betsy died in 1898 and there were many who argued that neither she nor any of those who went before her would be any the worse if they were moved to some more convenient spot.

Happily for the conservationists, the survival of this picturesque plot, with its fine wrought iron gates (made by G. Bunker about 1728) and its big old tombs – that of Richard Shaw, solicitor to Warren Hastings at the time of his trial, is still clearly visible above the wall in Court Lane – now looks more assured than it has done for some time.

With a history dating back at least as far as King Edgar, Dulwich probably derives its name from the old English 'dill' meaning 'white flower' and 'wihs' meaning 'damp meadow'. In other words it was 'the meadow where the white flower grows' and, like many of London's oldest villages, it became part of a Saxon royal estate which eventually passed into the hands of the Norman kings. The manor was given by Henry I in 1127 to the Cluniac monks of Bermondsey who kept it until it was seized by Henry VIII. Henry VIII presented it to goldsmith Thomas Calton whose grandson Francis sold it to Edward Alleyn in 1605 for nearly £5000.

When the rich actor decided to come and live here with his first wife, Joan Woodwarde, to whom he is said to have been most happily married for thirty-one years, nearly all the roads were country lanes and remained so for nearly three centuries. In fact, until about a hundred years ago, there were no real roads apart from the old High Street and its continuation (now College Road, formerly Morgan's Road), and no religious house apart from Alleyn's chapel. The church of St Barnabus, whose large square red brick tower (1908) one sees silhouetted against the sky just within the northernmost boundary of the conservation area near the top of Calton Avenue, was not built until 1894, which meant that churchgoers had to trek over the hill (now Calton Avenue, formerly Green- or Church Lane) to St Giles on the road to Camberwell.

There was however the traditional stocks and 'cage' and also a village pound for stray animals, all situated around the lower end of the hill. In recent years a stone, presumably once part of the 'cage' or lock-up, was found in a garden near the modern petrol station. It bore the date 1760 and the inscription: "It is a sport for a fool to do mischief. Thine own wickedness shall correct thee"!

The gallery bookshop marks the spot where the blacksmith's forge stood, while Gilkes Place just behind it was the site of the horse pond. Gilkes Place and Crescent were named after Arthur Herman Gilkes, Master of Dulwich College from 1885 to 1914.

The small listed property called Ash Cottage on the corner between Calton Avenue and Court Lane was built in 1814, nearly a hundred years before the appearance of the three pleasant residential roads running between Court Lane and Woodwarde Road. These three roads were built from 1909 onwards on farmland belonging to the College and are within the conservation area. Dekker Road was named after one of Alleyn's associates, a playwright of the early Stuart period; Desanfans Road after the art connoisseur through whom the college received most of its fine picture collection; and Druce Road after the family which produced a succession of holders of the office of Steward and Solicitor to the College Estate Governors from 1787 down to the present day.

As ground landlords, the estate governors have long been responsible for most of the rules concerning Dulwich's development and it is only recently, following the Leasehold Reform Bill, that they have made application (now approved by the High Court) whereby lease-holders can acquire their freeholds subject to certain conditions. However not all Dulwich residents are enthusiastic about the change, some fearing the effects which the loss of a co-ordinated policy for the control of buildings and trees could have.

Several recently built houses in the main street provide good examples of the care which so far has been taken to ensure harmony and continuity. In fact some have been so carefully matched with existing properties that it is not always easy to distinguish them from the genuine article. With its detached eighteenth-century coach house, No 57 Dulwich Village, standing just beyond the old cemetery, was built early in the nineteenth century and its neighbour No 59, though somewhat altered, a little earlier, but the remainder of this impressive three-storeyed terrace, Nos 61 to 67, is a modern addition.

By contrast, that conspicuous centre of local sociability, the 'Crown and Greyhound', has never made any attempt to look like anything other than what it is though its name and sign are an amalgam of two very old inns. The old 'Crown' stood on the site of the present Edwardian building and the much larger rambling old Greyhound Inn stood on the opposite (west) side of the road. The 'Greyhound' was demolished in 1898 to make way for Pickwick Road but in its heyday it was the rendezvous of many great literary figures, including Dickens, Thackeray and Ruskin, to whom its lucrative tea gardens were a special attraction. It was also a meeting place for the Dulwich Club to which most local 'gentlemen' subscribed.

All four of the residential roads in the triangle enclosed by Dulwich Village, Turney Road and Burbage Road were built on land which once belonged to the 'Greyhound', the earliest dwellings being the row of small eighteenth-century houses called Boxall Row, now incorporated into Boxall Road and named after Robert Boxall whose entrepreneurial activities were apparently not confined to the tap room.

Most of the cottages and small shops that line the main street on the west side are around two hundred years old and are on the scheduled list. At the lower end of the street on the corner facing the Hamlet Schools, the two-storeyed pair with the low pitched roof, Nos 50 and 52 Dulwich Village, appeared early in the nineteenth century, about the same time as some of the converted shop property higher up. The end terrace shop, No 70 (now selling antiques), is interesting because originally it was the saddlers, whereas the tiny amber brick house next door is reputedly the smallest house in Dulwich.

The group numbered 78 to 82 and also No 86 Dulwich Village belong to the eighteenth century though No 84 (now the sports shop), with its projecting canopy roof, is an early nineteenth-century building. Beneath the paintwork of Nos 94 and 96 (now occupied respectively by a travel agency and the London Steak House) is grey brick and with nineteenth-century stucco dressings.

Agewise, the elegant residential terraces beyond the post office on the east side of the street are an interesting mixture. Contrary to first impressions, the attractive pair Nos 93 and

95, named North House and South House, were built in recent times, though the magnificent group that follows, Nos 97 to 105, is very much the genuine article. In fact this group of houses, with its beautiful doorways, has remained virtually unchanged since the eighteenth-century.

But inevitably at this point the attention becomes diverted from Georgian architecture to the splendid pile at the elbow junction in the middle of the road between College Road and Gallery Road. Now popularly known as 'Old College', this was the original building of the school which Edward Alleyn founded and which received its charter from James I in 1619 – the school destined eventually to become Dulwich College. The coat of arms on the early wrought iron gates at the entrance to the forecourt – originally the site of the village green – was adopted by Alleyn from his mother's family.

All three ranges around the forecourt have been restored or extended but they still faithfully reflect much of the original building put up by John Benson on behalf of the founder. For some reason an architect was not employed.

The east wing was rebuilt in 1740 and 1866 but it is still used, as intended, as almshouses for old people. The west wing was extended in 1820 and again in modern times and now serves as the office of the estate governors. It was in the west wing that Alleyn's "twelve poor scholars" and their few paying companions received their education.

With its nineteenth-century additions, including the tower and the cloister, the central (south) range, still formally known as Christ's Chapel of Alleyn's College of God's Gift, continues to fulfil its original purpose as the chapel of the scholastic community (consisting nowadays of Dulwich College, Alleyn's School and James Allen's Girls' School) and of the almspeople and the inhabitants of the "hamlet of Dulwich".

The somewhat quaint name given to the chapel arises from an original ruling of the foundation. According to this ruling, whenever there were two boys of equal eligibility competing for one place in the school, the boys had to draw lots from two pieces of paper, only one of which was inscribed with the words "God's Gift" – a useful device no doubt for placing the onus of choice upon the divinity, especially in view of the final lines of the Latin inscription above the entrance to the chapel pointing out that "Blessed is he who has taken pity on the poor. Go thou and do likewise"!

Although Edward Alleyn lies buried in the chapel in front of the altar, the black marble stone which at present covers his tomb was not placed there until 1816. The original stone was discovered earlier this century in the yard of the Half Moon Inn and erected in the cloisters in 1925.

The present reredos (screen behind the altar) was erected in 1911 and depicts two boy attendants in the school uniform of Alleyn's day. Another reminder of those far-off days comes at the end of every service when a prayer is said giving "humble and hearty thanks for the memory in this place of Edward Alleyn, our Founder and Benefactor, by whose godliness this whole college is brought up to godliness and good learning".

For two centuries however the "good learning" was restricted to only a handful of boys, for, despite Alleyn's high ambitions as expressed in his statutes, the grand project was overthrown and it was not until 1858, following an Act of Parliament, that a big reorganisation took place.

Nevertheless the intriguing little early Victorian one-storey structure now known as the Old Grammar School, which stands on the corner site on the opposite side of Gallery Road, had already appeared, in about 1842. With its gabled ends, steeply pitched roof and Tudor-style chimneys, this tiny building was founded by the college as an additional school

Old Grammar School

and was designed by no less a person than Sir Charles Barry who later became famous as the architect of the Houses of Parliament. Unfortunately, after a somewhat inglorious history, the Old Grammar School had to close its doors as such, having been replaced under the new college charter of 1858 by what is now Alleyn's School in Townley Road (outside the conservation area). For a long time the Old Grammar School building was used as a reading room but it now serves as a meeting place for local societies and for playgroups.

The old milestone which stands on the island refuge near the drinking fountain in the forefront of this unique Dulwich scene dates back to about 1772 and the message of its somewhat illegible inscription still holds good: "V miles from the Treasury, V miles from Standard Corner".

The other remarkable building here in the centre of Dulwich only five miles from central London is of course the famous Dulwich Picture Gallery. As its College Road frontage, set back amid green lawns and fine trees, comes into view just beyond the almshouses, it is worth remembering that this is the oldest public gallery in England. Unmistakable by its yellow brick walls and neo-Greek style, it owes its existence to the art connoisseur Noel Desanfans, the man who responded to a request to collect pictures for King Stanislaus of Poland only to find the fruits of his searches left suddenly on his hands when the king abdicated in 1795. After Desanfans had failed to persuade the British Government to buy the pictures as the basis for a National Gallery, he finally bequeathed them to his wife Margaret and to his friend Sir Francis Bourgeois, who in turn left them to Dulwich College on condition that they were put on show to the public. Margaret Desanfans gave £6000 to have a special gallery built for them.

The gallery was built in 1811-14 by the architect Sir John Soane and opened in 1817. With its projecting wings and mausoleum on axis – the mausoleum contains the remnants of Sir Francis Bourgeois and both the Desanfans – it suffered severe damage during the Second World War but was rebuilt almost exactly to the original Soane designs. The large glazed portions of the low pitched roof are intended to provide top lighting, as they were in Soane's day, for the series of galleries which still house some fine collections of seventeenth- and eighteenth-century art. This was the gallery that achieved so much notoriety in December 1966 when eight of its masterpieces, including works by Rembrandt and Rubens, were stolen in a daring robbery. Fortunately the pictures were later recovered.

In the earliest days of the village, College Road was just a rough track across the common leading from Dulwich to Penge but in 1804 it was laid down as a private road. It acquired its present name in 1870 when the new college buildings were erected farther along. Today the grass verges and side paths, with their protective white posts and link chains, reflect some of the efforts made to preserve the village atmosphere and to protect the pedestrian. Obviously the incursions of the motorist are still a problem, though this middle region of the conservation area is fortunate in having the 72-acre Dulwich Park (opened in 1890 on a farmland site made over by the estate governors to the London County Council) on its eastern flank. The boundary crosses the entrance to the park.

Nearly every house on the east side of College Road is of some interest. The three-storeyed group numbered eleven to fifteen were all built in Georgian times and No 15's lead fire insurance plate, still there on the creeper-covered wall, is a reminder of the days when public fire brigades were virtually non-existent and insurance companies such as the Sun sent their own engines to the properties of those who paid the premium.

The square, white-painted, weather-boarded house with the shutters and tiled roof called Bell Cottage was also built in the eighteenth century and is one of the few survivors of its kind in this part of London. Enormous Bell House (No 27) just beyond was built in 1767 and is now a junior boarding-house for Dulwich College. The bell on the roof was formerly used as a village fire alarm.

Pickwick Cottage, No 31 College Road, is believed to be the house which Dickens had in mind for the retirement of his famous character in *Pickwick Papers*. At the end of the story, Mr Pickwick comes to live in Dulwich where he was "frequently seen contemplating the pictures in the Dulwich Gallery". Before it rose to fame in this way, Pickwick Cottage was simply Grove Cottage, taking its name from the footpath called 'The Grove' that links College Road to Gallery Road and runs alongside the playing fields opposite.

These fields were formerly part of a large meadow known since time immemorial as Howlett's Green. Like the common itself, such greens and clearings were a special feature of medieval Dulwich.

The large group of modern 'town' houses called College

Gardens was a replacement development for eight yellow-brick Victorian mansions built in 1860 on the site of the old Fellows' Garden belonging to the College. The brick pier with the Victorian post-box near the entrance drive is a relic of the earlier development.

As one approaches the traffic artery called Dulwich Common, now part of London's South Circular route (A 205), it is interesting to remember that this was once an important stretch of the Pilgrim's Way which led from the Thames ferries to Canterbury.

The conservation area includes virtually the whole length of Dulwich Common, from just short of Queen Mary's Gate (Dulwich Park) almost to West Dulwich Station. The house called Oakfield at the corner with College Road (one frontage facing Dulwich Common) dates back to the early eighteenth century, and so does the Old Blew House about half way between College Road and Gallery Road. The Old Blew House is of some historical interest because in 1626 Edward Alleyn bequeathed the site on which it stands to the poor of his native parish, St Botolph's, Bishopsgate.

The conspicuous but neglected-looking white stuccoed Victorian mansion called Hambleden House on the south side of the road at the eastern extremity of the conservation area was used for several years as a nurses' home – until controversy and argument over its future left it without an occupant.

Fortunately no such problems confront the small group of old cottages facing the Mill Pond on the south side of Dulwich Common. With its ducks and overhanging trees, this area has always been a haunt of artists and, over the years, it is believed that Pond Cottages, including the diminutive weather-boarded No 4, have provided shelter for many portrayers of the local scene. Perhaps the best known was the eighteenth-century landscape artist David Cox who occupied one of the cottages for a time.

In those days, the opposite side of College Road (now occupied by Dulwich College) consisted of a last remnant of common land (not enclosed by the estate governors until 1805) and on it, at the corner, stood the old Dulwich windmill – a familiar feature of many of the old landscapes.

Although not to everybody's taste – some people see them as smaller versions of St Pancras Station! – the large red-brick buildings in fourteenth-century northern Italian style that

Dulwich College

dominate the west side of College Road are a basic part of the famous school. They were built in 1870 by Charles Barry, son of the architect of the Houses of Parliament, and at the time were claimed to be among the most commodious and complete fabrics built for educational purposes that century. They were also among the most costly and, hardly surprisingly, by the time the controversial modern science block was placed in their midst, there was no hope of matching or competing with them.

In order to take in the old tollgate, the conservation area extends a further short distance southward along College Road. The tollgate was set up in 1789 by Charles Morgan of Penge after he decided to build a road to provide easier access to some fields which he had rented from the College. His intention was simply to recoup some of the money he had spent.

After Morgan died, the college kept the gate and went on charging tolls to defray the cost of its upkeep – as indeed they still do. The gate survived the Act of Parliament of 1864 which abolished most of its kind and it is now the only one left in London. The old list of charges on the board beside the road tells its own story both as regards the changing value of money and the changing nature of road users, though today's motor

Old Tollgate

car costs a modest 3p and there is no charge at night.

The conservation area boundary follows the long and verdant peripheral roads called Hunts Slip Road and Alleyn Park which enclose the Dulwich College campus and bring one back to Dulwich Common nearly opposite the northern end of Gallery Road.

Although most of the recreational ground flanking Gallery Road is privately owned, the land belonging to the solitary grey stuccoed mansion called 'Belair' on the west side now belongs to the general public.

Originally known as College Place, Belair was built in 1785 and, as the plaque on the wall of the entrance lodge explains, it remained a private residence until 1938. By 1947 however, Belair had become almost derelict and it was leased by Southwark Borough Council for sport and recreation. Since then the house has undergone complete renovation, leaving only the fine central staircase intact. It is this staircase, together with the round central bay and ground floor terrace with Ionic columns at the rear which has caused it to be attributed to Robert Adam, though it is still thought possible that the designer was Henry Holland. In 1967 Belair was the scene of the Dulwich Millennium (thousand years of history) celebrations.

The attractive long lake at the bottom of Belair's grounds, lying just within the boundary of the conservation area west of Gallery Road, is believed to be a branch of the long lost River Effra, now mainly hidden underground – a fitting place perhaps to pause and be grateful that Dulwich Village escaped the fate that befell its ancient river and became instead one of London's outstanding conservation areas.

4

Enfield Town

Market Place and Church of St Andrew

Perhaps one of the pleasantest things about Enfield town is the feeling that if the eighteenth-century gentlemen of Gentleman's Row came back today they might still recognise their whereabouts. Not only might they recognise the fascinating row of houses where once they lived in the leafy enclave near the banks of the famous man-made New River, but also the quaint old lanes along which they used to lead their progeny to church.

Perhaps it is the church which explains the puzzle of how this old Middlesex town has managed to retain so many pockets of interest and charm when all around it villages have degenerated into unrecognisable north London suburbs. St Andrew's has occupied its acre and a half of ground on the north side of the central market-place for close on seven centuries and, squeezed and dwarfed though it now is by the

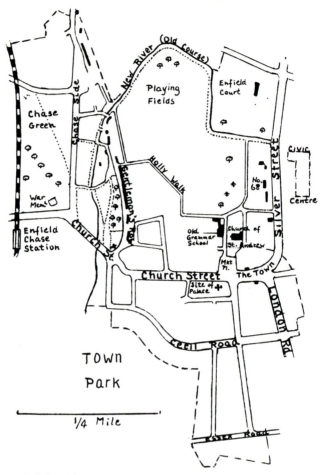

commercial buildings around its frontage, it still shows no
sign of yielding. Such tenacity must surely have its own
reward so who can wonder if it continues to cast its spell over
the network of narrow lanes and paths which still shelter
behind it? Certainly the old church holds the key to much of
the story of what is now the Enfield town conservation area.

The story may have begun in prehistoric times but even by
the time the Romans built Ermine Street about a mile to the
east, Enfield was still only a clearing in the forest. Later on,
under the Saxons, it became a hamlet in the Hundred of

Edmonton and it was this hamlet which turned itself into the village of Geoffrey de Mandeville's time. Geoffrey de Mandeville was the Norman landlord who, in about 1190, acquired the manor and laid the foundations of the church, several small parts of which still survive.

The church was an added attraction for the wealthy people who were beginning to come to hunt in the forest and in 1303 Edward I granted Enefelde, as it was then called, two annual fairs (finally demolished in 1869) and a weekly market – the forerunner of today's familiar and colourful bazaar with its canopied stalls.

Evidence of the next stage of Enfield's development can actually be seen in the church. By the time the manor had been inherited by the wife of the future Henry IV and had become part of the Duchy of Lancaster, it was already attracting some of the newly rich London merchants, many of whom were anxious to act as benefactors or to leave their mark in some way. None of the country houses built by these wealthy newcomers survive but the finely preserved brass altar tomb which still stands intact on the north side of the sanctuary provides a striking example of the period. It is the tomb of the Lady Jacosa Tiptoft, daughter of Baron Charlton de Powys and wife of a famous soldier, who died in 1446.

With the help of its new benefactors, the church reached its present form and size by the end of the sixteenth century, after which it remained virtually unaltered until 1823.

But beyond the church, Enfield's connections with the royal family were being strengthened. A few miles to the north, Elsynge Hall (later known as Enfield Hall but demolished in 1629 by Sir Nicholas Raynton after he had built Forty Hall) was acquired by Henry VIII and became the home of Elizabeth I and her younger brother Edward during some of their early years. It was from this house that Edward VI's accession to the throne was announced in 1547 – a ceremony to be echoed three and a half centuries later in Enfield's market-place at the time of the coronation of his descendant, Edward VII.

Under her father's Will, Elizabeth received the adjoining manors of Enfield and Worcesters and later occasionally held her court at Elsynge, but there is no evidence that she ever stayed at the old Tudor Palace (finally demolished in 1928) that stood on Enfield Green, the now unoccupied site on the south side of Church Street opposite the market-place.

Like Elizabeth before him, James I used to come to hunt occasionally at Enfield Chase but after he died royal interest appears to have declined and there are now only a few reminders of those times. The colourful marble memorial to Sir Nicholas Raynton, builder of Forty Hall, which still occupies the north-east corner of the church is probably the most important surviving one. Depicted here in full armour, with his wife beneath him contemplating the Ten Commandments and followed by more distant members of the family in a variety of postures, Sir Nicholas died in 1646.

The magnificent organ case at the west end of the church was installed in 1751. By this time urbanisation was setting in and several of the houses in Gentleman's Row, Enfield Chase and Silver Street had already made their appearance – a fact which contributed to the demand for alterations to the church. The present south aisle and porch were rebuilt in 1823 to match the north aisle and also, unfortunately, the stucco or Roman cement that still covers the original flint rubble on the north and east faces was applied. This particular innovation seems to have aroused the disapproval of Enfield's celebrated resident Charles Lamb, for when he wrote to Wordsworth in 1830 he referred to the "new plastered flat church".

Many of the encroachments around the frontage of the church came with the Victorian building boom – a boom which culminated in the replacement of the old Market House by the present open octagonal structure in the middle of the market-place. With its eight teak pillars emulating its predecessor's oak ones, the Market House was erected by public subscription to commemorate the coronation of Edward VII after the proclamation of his accession in 1901 and was used for the special ceremony based on the proclamation of Edward VI's accession in 1547.

The well preserved two-storey old grammar school building in Church Walk near the market-place dates back to 1586. With its warm red Tudor brick and steeply tiled dormered roof, it owes its existence to a certain William Garrett who left £50 for its construction in order that the chantry school, founded in 1557, could be given a permanent home and offer the boys of Enfield a general education. The ground floor consists of one large school-room (50 feet by 21 feet but now partitioned) which, although now a minor adjunct to the extensive present-day premises of Enfield Grammar School, is still used for teaching and form-room purposes. No addition

Old Grammar School building

was made to the sixteenth-century building until 1739-40 when some refitting took place. Nowadays most of the windows are modern, though each of the three gabled dormers possesses a partly restored original window, as does the semi-octagonal stair on the other side (west front).

The picturesque looking house at the corner of Church Walk and Holly Walk, made up of Uvedale House and Uvedale Cottage, is where Dr Robert Uvedale, headmaster of the school from 1664 to 1676 lived. As well as being one of the grammar school's most famous headmasters, Dr Uvedale was known as a great plant lover and achieved remembrance as the introducer of sweet peas into the country from Sicily.

History does not relate which of the two routes from this corner of Holly Walk Dr Uvedale favoured when setting out on his country walks – the left-hand westerly route in the direction of the New River or the equally inviting easterly route around the old churchyard towards the vicarage and Silver Street. No doubt then, as now, the choice presented something of a dilemma.

Even in Dr Uvedale's day the old yew, now believed to be four hundred years old, must have been a significant feature of the huge vicarage garden. The Elizabethan house itself however was transformed in early Georgian times and now only a few of the original features, including the old Tudor beams and window frames, remain.

Several of the houses above the vicarage in Silver Street, notably Nos 58, 60 and 68, are Grade 2 listed properties. The large white weather-boarded house with the projecting two-storey porch, numbered 68 and now used as a doctor's surgery, was built in the eighteenth century and eventually became the home, from 1862 onwards, of the publisher and almanack compiler, Joseph Whitaker (1820-1895). The recently restored No 90, with its Doric door and pediment, was built in the late eighteenth century.

No 68 Silver Street

Enfield Court, the large brick house with the green slate roof and parapet which stands well back in spacious grounds farther up this main street, is now occupied by Enfield Grammar School's junior department. It was built in 1690 (southern wing rebuilt 1864) and once belonged to the original manor of Worcesters. Close to its southern boundary where the course of the New River still flows, there was once an old gazebo and circular riding school built by Sir Alfred Somerset.

Unfortunate though it is, it seems that none of these houses on the conservation area's eastern boundary can now escape the long shadows of the massive tower block of the new Civic Centre on the opposite side of the road – a spectre which, however admirable in itself, appears likely to dominate the eastern skyline for as long as anybody can foresee. All the more reason therefore, if one returns southward via Silver Street to the semi-circular junction known as The Town, for feeling grateful that there were technical limits to what the Victorians could do when they replaced the original wooden shops that once stood grouped around this busy central corner.

The only wooden building to survive here is the late seventeenth-century gabled and weather-boarded house, No 3-4 The Town (at present painted white with green window frames and with a carpet shop on the ground floor), on the south side of the street.

No 22 The Town, or the old vestry offices as it is still sometimes called, which stands near the corner of the market-place opposite, is listed for a different reason. Hemmed in between a shoe shop and a bank, this quaint little one-storey hexagonal structure of brown brick with stone and stucco dressings was built early in the nineteenth-century for use as a beadle's office and later became a police station with a 'cage' on either side for malefactors.

Almost the whole of the residential area south of The Town's continuation road, Church Street, including Palace Gardens named after the old Tudor Palace that stood close by, is a legacy from the Victorian era. Set well back in its pleasant precinct at the end of the Church Street shops, the public library was built in 1894.

Area-wise, however, most of the territory of the conservation area lies to the north-west where the New River pursues its meandering course through gardens and open fields – territory bounded on the west by Chase Green and on the north by the old course of the river itself. Approached from Church Street via Little Park Gardens just behind the Methodist church, this is the world of Gentleman's Row and those other peaceful enclaves where thresholds are still separated from the motor car by narrow footpaths and intervening plantations of private gardens and trees.

The large elongated house, now used as council offices, which stands alone behind the open forecourt at the beginning of Gentleman's Row belongs to the late eighteenth century. It is in fact much older than its secluded neighbour, No 5, whose clock is just visible above the high wall as one begins to penetrate the hidden delights of the celebrated footpath. Although No 5, otherwise known as Little Park, retains some

Gentleman's Row

sixteenth-century work, it has been mostly rebuilt and its major interest now lies in the special room on the south side formed out of fittings taken from the old Tudor Palace at the time of its demolition in 1928. The fittings consist mainly of panelling and a stone fireplace *circa* 1552.

The two-storeyed brick Elm House with the attractive railings in front belongs to the eighteenth century, though it could, like its stucco-fronted neighbour Fortescue House (No 11) be older than that. It is thought possible that at one time nearly all the houses in Gentleman's Row had parapeted façades, the dormered windows being added at a later date in the prevailing style of the day.

As the plaque indicates, the white weather-boarded Coach House is believed to have begun life as a sixteenth-century barn in which animals were kept for the hunt. In fact the outlines of some of the old stables still exist inside this house.

The three-storeyed pair, Nos 13 and 15, built in yellow brick and recently restored in Georgian style with slatted shutters, were built in 1840-50, which means that they were not there when Charles and Mary Lamb came in 1825 and again in 1827 to stay with their friends the Allsops at Clarendon Cottage before making their decision to settle locally. However the neighbouring houses Nos 19 and 21 on the north side of Clarendon Cottage had already been built. With their fluted doorcases, both these houses date back to the early eighteenth century, about a quarter of a century before No 23, with its fine dark yellow brick and adjoining elliptical archway, appeared.

By the time one reaches this point where the footpath opens out, one may well have lost count of the number of bronze plaques which today adorn the porches or walls of the houses of Gentleman's Row. To mark European Heritage Year (1975), these insignia were commissioned and supplied by the Enfield Preservation Society for use on properties of architectural or historic interest and all are voluntarily displayed by the owners or occupiers. The declared objective of the exercise was to encourage pride and awareness among local residents and the scheme is now being extended to include most of Enfield's listed properties. At this northern end of Gentleman's Row, The Haven (No 16), the early nineteenth-century Rivulet House (No 32) and the neglected mid-eighteenth-century Brecon House (No 55) that stands behind wrought iron gates in its extensive river-facing garden are among those on the scheduled list.

As one crosses the footbridge into what might almost be mistaken for some old Venetian backwater, it is interesting to reflect that when the old course of the New River was built and completed in 1613, few people saw it as a laudable enterprise, either aesthetically or from a practical point of view.

With its source in the Chadwell Springs between Hertford and Ware and with its head at Islington, the river was built for the purpose of bringing pure water from the wells to seventeenth-century London. Yet so persistent was the opposition that the promoter, Sir Hugh Myddleton, who lived at the top of Bush Hill in a house called 'Halliwick' not far from Enfield Town, ended up by sinking a personal fortune on the project. Nevertheless, by the time the river was straightened in the nineteenth century, attitudes had changed and the old meandering course that still winds its way through this part of Enfield, adding so much to the charm of the conservation area, was left alone. Today not only are its scenic qualities appreciated but the whole picturesque construction is regarded as a remarkable feat of engineering.

Originally few buildings appear to have been erected close to the water but it is thought that the house with its own small footbridge on the east bank known as 'The Laurels' could well have been built on the site of an older house. Alternatively, its stuccoed eighteenth- or early nineteenth-century façade could have been added to an earlier building already there.

Nobody seems to know exactly when the 'Coach and Horses' first established itself in the bend where the waterway sharply changes direction after its long perambulation across the fields from Silver Street. However it is an old inn and it is now included in the scheduled list.

Chase Side, into which one emerges from the network of lanes north of Horseshoe Lane, contains yet another long string of listed properties, starting with the small group numbered 77 to 83, built early in the nineteenth century, and followed by the weather-boarded cottage, No 85, which is about a hundred years older.

From the point of view of literary association, the somewhat neglected-looking No 87 Chase Side is of special interest. Although considerably modified in later years, this house was built early in the nineteenth century and it was here that the poet and essayist Charles Lamb first settled with his sister in 1827. Charles and Mary Lamb lived at No 87 for two years before moving to the more attractive No 89 next door at the invitation of their neighbours, the Westwoods, who had undertaken to help care for Mary, a sufferer from recurring bouts of mental illness. It was in the back sitting-room of Westwood Cottage that Charles Lamb wrote *Essays of Elia* before disillusionment with the elderly Westwoods made him decide to move to Edmonton in 1833.

It is interesting to recall that, as a child, the poet John Keats (1795-1821) also knew Enfield town very well, first as a pupil at the boarding-school to which he came daily from Edmonton and then as a frequent visitor of his friend and tutor, Charles Cowden Clarke, son of the headmaster.

The cottages numbered 93, 95 and 97 are believed, despite their nineteenth-century frontages, to date back possibly as far as the late seventeenth century, while No 103 whose frontage abuts on to the pavement opposite Christ Church was built some fifty years later.

Standing at this northern tip of the conservation area and conspicuous by its graceful spire, Christ Church was founded as a Congregational church in 1780 by a London merchant who came to live in Enfield and opened his house on the sabbath to friends and neighbours.

All the open land called Chase Green to the west of Chase Side, with the war memorial at its southern end, is designated territory. As the name suggests, this pleasant parkland, with its present-day clumps of trees and pathways leading one back through riverside gardens to within sight of Gentleman's Row, once stood on the edge of the great hunting forest where people came in the early days of Enfield's history.

If one returns to the market-place from Gentleman's Row via the old flagged footpath, Holly Walk, one can hardly ignore the twentieth-century tower of the modern borough's civic centre as it zooms into view on the distant skyline. Yet there still comes, at almost every turn, that fresh whiff of the old country town which is surely the essence of this extensive and unexpectedly charming conservation area.

Forty Hill

The giant concrete plant pots now standing sentinel across the main road to protect Forty Hill from onrushing traffic seems like a great divide, providing a sudden transition from north London's built-up suburbia to what is still virtually open country.

This hilly and exhilarating conservation area with its long backbone of charming old houses and fine Jacobean mansion, its hinterland of trees, streams and ponds, and its ancient continuation road, Bull's Cross, once formed the slopes of the great forest on to which Elizabeth, the Tudor princess, and her young brother Edward used to look out from one of their childhood homes, Elsynge Hall.

Later known as Enfield House, Elsynge Hall was acquired by Henry VIII and in 1547 was the scene of the announcement of Edward VI's accession to the throne. From all accounts, the royal children never forgot it and even in later years Elizabeth I used sometimes to come back and hold her court here. The house continued to exist until after 1629 when the wealthy haberdasher, Sir Nicholas Raynton, replaced it by Forty Hall.

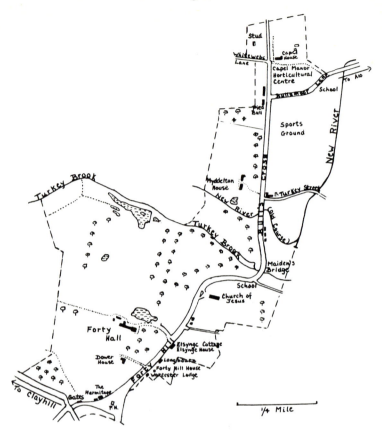

Once the new Jacobean mansion had been established, a variety of lesser dwellings gradually made their appearance alongside the main roads and it is these houses, or relics of them, which survive today and make such an important contribution to the Forty Hill conservation area.

If one starts at the south-eastern tip at the bottom of the hill where small groups of flats and a row of shops have replaced the wooden smithy and the old plantations, one may well wonder about the pair of fine gates and railings which face the road yet appear to lead nowhere except into a thicket of trees and saplings. The answer is that these late seventeenth- or early eighteenth-century gates once formed the entrance to Gough Park – a house occupied for a long time by an antiquarian writer called Richard Gough who died in 1809. About 1860 the course of the New River was changed and the gates and railings of Gough Park were thrown forward by a later owner so as to include an offshoot of the old river bed. However in 1899 Gough Park was demolished and eventually even the stretch of old water course that ran through the grounds was filled up, leaving nothing but the gates as a reminder of the old house. Recognising their interest and value, the London Borough of Enfield restored them in 1975.

The gates that lead nowhere

The charming red brick house with the dormered roof known as The Hermitage, No 78 Forty Hill, standing just above the group of late Victorian cottages on the north side of the road where the land begins to rise, dates back to 1714. The Victorian blind fascias were added later.

As in so many conservation areas, the survival rate of old names is high and the origins are often easy to guess at. As one might expect, the neo-Tudor public house conspicuous on its triangular site opposite 'The Hermitage' is called after an old inn. The original 'Goat' was a wooden structured building with overhanging storey that stood across Goat Lane a little higher up the road. Yellow-brick Cannister House, on the other hand, owes its name to its resemblance to a tea cannister. Built in the early nineteenth-century arcaded style, this house originally had a stuccoed front.

Red-brick Worcester Lodge and also the gabled and timbered Dower House, which can just be seen at the end of the driveway on the opposite (west) side of the road, belong to the early eighteenth century, whereas Forty Hill House and Longbourn were built about a century later.

Several of these listed houses, including attractive Elsynge House and adjoining Elsynge Cottage (named after Elsynge Hall of Elizabethan times) lost their front gardens when the footway was widened about seventy years ago. The Elsynge pair, with their ground floor Venetian windows, date back to the early eighteenth century. Among others on the scheduled list are Waltham Cottage and Sparrow Hall which stand just north of the nursery gardens and massive late Victorian (1893) roadside Clock House (now let out as flats).

Forty Hall itself, with its main drive immediately opposite the Victorian mansion, was acquired by the council in 1951, since which time the informal gardens with their long avenue of limes, ancient Lebanon cedars and fine oaks – the oaks are said to be descendants of those which formed the ancient forest of Middlesex – have been open to the public. Extensive restorations to the actual mansion began in 1962 and by 1966 this too was re-opened. Since then the outbuildings have been adapted to form a reception area for the benefit of visitors to the various art, furniture and local history exhibitions which are now regularly held there.

With one of its three classical façades looking out on to the attractive small lake and avenue of limes, the 'square-box'

Forty Hall

mansion has been attributed both to Inigo Jones and to his assistant John Webb but nobody seems able to prove with any certainty that either was responsible. The arched brick gateway that leads to the seventeenth-century kitchen court is usually quoted as a very good example of the influence of Inigo Jones.

After Sir Nicholas Raynton died in 1646 – his colourful tomb is in Enfield Church – there was a succession of owners, at least two of whom carried out repairs, modernisations and alterations, including eventually the plastering of the mansion's internal walls. Happily for posterity, the exuberant seventeenth-century plaster ceilings and some of the fine panelling were left intact.

Beyond the group of ponds, the northern boundary of the park, marked by Turkey Brook, forms part of the boundary of this south-eastern section of the conservation area. Turkey Brook is the stream one sees passing under narrow hump-backed Maiden's Bridge after the winding road has taken one up past Jesus Church (built in 1835 by Thomas Ashwell) and past the local primary school. It eventually finds its way into the River Lea.

At Maiden's Bridge, where the road continues northwards but changes its name from Forty Hill to Bull's Cross, one may stop to wonder why the bends and curves have suddenly disappeared. The answer is as straight and simple as Bull's Cross itself. Originally this road was part of the Roman Ermine Street and a ruler placed on a large map will indicate how it once linked up with what is now the Great Cambridge Road (A 10). It acquired its present name of Bull's Cross from Bedelles Cross, an old landmark dating back to medieval times which used to stand at a fourway crossing at the top of the hill where Whitewebs Lane still joins it.

The second stream to pass under the main road (just north of the old cottages on the east side of Bull's Cross) is the old course of the New River. No doubt this additional waterway was seen as an added attraction and probably accounts for the three beautifully kept white stuccoed houses built in the late eighteenth century which still stand at this end of Turkey Street.

The straightened version of the New River, into which the old course makes its way, forms much of the conservation areas' eastern boundary. This is the man-made river which one sees passing under Turkey Street and which runs almost parallel to Bull's Cross as far as Bullsmoor Lane, thereby taking in the various sports grounds and other stretches of open land on the east side.

Myddelton House, on the west side of Bull's Cross opposite the end of Turkey Street, is a good example of a large country house that has found a valuable modern usage. Now a medical school, this late eighteenth-century yellow brick mansion with its splendid views was formerly the home of a landscape gardener and horticulturist called E.A. Bowles (no relation to the last private owners of Forty Hall of the same name) who laid out the flagged gardens with exotic plants and old-fashioned roses. The handsome stable block coach-house with the circular clock turret on the north side of the house was built in the early nineteenth century.

The weather-boarded and stuccoed but much altered Pied Bull public house, which stands just above Myddelton Farm and dates back to the late seventeenth or early eighteenth century, is also on the scheduled list (grade 3), and so is the house called 'The Orchards' higher up.

However it is the splendid Capel Manor Horticultural Centre on the east side of the road, with its main entrance in Bullsmoor Lane, that accounts for most of this northern end of the conservation area. After the council acquired the thirty-

Capel Manor Horticultural Institute

acre estate in 1967, it was developed for the teaching of horticulture to vocational and non-vocational students, though the grounds are frequently thrown open to the general public during the summer. The copper beeches in the woodland area are said to be originals of the species introduced into the country two hundred years ago, while the pool beyond the spacious walled gardens is of natural formation.

Another interesting feature of Capel Manor is the quality of the twentieth-century stable buildings, with their clock tower and weather-vane bearing the figure of a horse. The last private owner was a Colonel Medcalf who bred Clydesdale horses.

Originally this estate was part of the manor of Capels and was named after Sir Giles Capels who transferred it to the Crown in 1547. After Elizabeth I had sold the manor back into private ownership, it passed through several hands before eventually being bought, in 1793, by an elderly Governor of Bombay called Rawson Hart Boddam. It was Boddam, after his second marriage, who built the present red-brick mansion as a home for himself and his ever-growing family and transferred to it the name of the handsome old manor house near by, which he pulled down. With its green slate roof, Boddam's late eighteenth-century mansion is now used by the Middlesex Polytechnic.

If one returns to Bull's Cross via the driveway that lies to the west of the house opposite the end of Whitewebs Lane, it is interesting to remind oneself that it was from the four-way crossing just ahead that the name of Bull's Cross was derived. In the days when it was still Bedelles Cross, before the original Capel House was built and the estate enclosed, the road from Whitewebs cut straight across the main road.

Even now there is an air of unchangeability about the top of the hill where the old medieval landmark once stood and where people must have drawn breath before starting out down the long narrow highways in the direction of London.

5

Greenwich

Flamsteed House

(i) GREENWICH PARK

In terms of sheer architectural splendour it is doubtful whether any other conservation area can match Greenwich Park. Bounded on the north side by that famous bend in the river made instantly recognisable by Wren's noble edifice (originally the Royal Hospital, now the Royal Naval College), it extends right up the steep green slope of the park past the Palladian-style Queen's House, with its nineteenth-century wings and linking colonnades (now the National Maritime Museum), as far as the Old Royal Observatory and beyond.

Both Maze Hill on the east and Croom's Hill on the west side of Greenwich Park are ancient ways and today Croom's

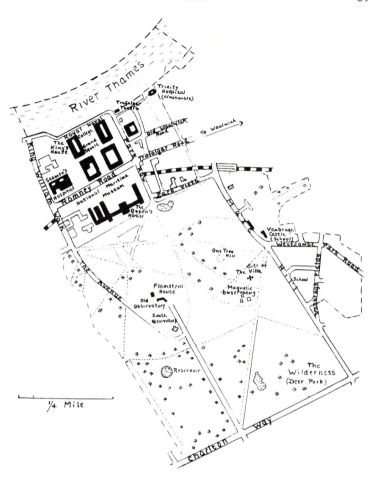

Hill forms a natural demarcation line between Greenwich Park and its neighbouring conservation area, West Greenwich.

The story of the whole area goes back of course a very long way and, although much is now accepted as reliable 'history', Greenwich still lives up to its reputation as a place of rumour and local legend. Not all its mysteries have yet been cleared up and one recent theory, supported by accumulated archaeological and documentary evidence, is that Greenwich was Trinovantum, the prehistoric capital of England near which Julius Caesar defeated the ancient Britons. The theory is that a great flood, due perhaps to a tidal wave, destroyed an important crossing into Essex, thereby reducing the strategic value of Greenwich and allowing it to be superseded by London.

But whether or not it was once an important capital or merely a small fishing settlement, everyone agrees that by the time the Saxons took it over, Greenwich – or Gronovic as it was then called – had become a prosperous trading port. King Alfred gave it, probably as a marriage portion, to his youngest daughter Elstrudis who in due course handed it over to the abbey at Ghent as a memorial to her husband. The old Abbot's House, dating back to these times, stood beside the river and was the first of the succession of houses to be built on the site where the Royal Hospital was founded in 1694.

If one arrives in Greenwich by water, the famous landmark lies only a short walk eastward from the pier along the river wall. After passing the King Charles' Building which John Webb designed for Charles II in 1662 as a replacement for a derelict wing of the old Tudor palace, there it is – the massive gates of the central courtyard (known as Grand Square) giving a clear close-up view of the twin domes of the Painted Hall and Chapel, with the Queen's House in the centre background and even part of the old observatory visible in the distance at the top of the hill. This was the scene that Canaletto painted from the opposite bank in about 1755 – a scene now regarded as the most unaltered in London.

To add to the fascination of it all, excavations carried out in 1971 in the central courtyard confirmed the one-time existence of the three earlier palaces. Included in the discoveries were the archaeological remains of the Abbot's House of Saxon times, of the Bella Court built as a country house in 1430 by Henry V's brother, Duke Humphrey, and of the Tudor palace of Pleasaunce, later called Placentia, which was built by Henry VI by adding on to Bella Court. It was at the Palace of Placentia, the most favoured of all Tudor royal residences, that Henry VIII, Mary I and Elizabeth I were born, and here too that the orders for resisting the Spanish Armada were signed.

Most of the present buildings were designed during the reign of William and Mary. The great naval victory over the French in 1692 inspired the Queen to turn the King's House (King Charles' Building) into a hospital for disabled and aged naval pensioners similar to that already established for soldiers at Chelsea by Charles II and to have the rest of Placentia rebuilt for the same purpose.

Wren's original scheme for first clearing the whole site was, however, rejected. The Queen wanted to keep both the King's House and the Queen's House and was equally adamant about retaining a 115-foot wide clearing between the Queen's House and the river in order to preserve the view. So Wren's hospital was an architectural compromise, with the buildings on the eastward side specially designed to balance the King's House on the west, and the consequent creation of the Grand Square. Wren also had to take into account the 'five foot walk' along the river wall – the walk that still takes one past the whole splendid façade to the end of Park Row. After it had been conceded that this was and must remain a right of way, the architect had no alternative but to scrap his original plan for close balustrading.

It was not until 1873, after the naval pensioners had been given means of self-support, that Wren's masterpiece was turned into the Royal Naval College – a college now used to provide higher education for officers.

Royal Naval College and Queen's House

The handsome Regency-style Trafalgar Tavern which comes right up to the water's edge on the corner of Park Row was built in 1837, the year Queen Victoria came to the throne. After some restoration in the early 1960s, it looks almost exactly as it did then, though at that time there were no giant chimneys just beyond it to mar the skyline. Unbelievable as it may seem, the electric power station (built in 1905 to power London's trams) was actually erected on the prime meridian! This unfortunate creation is, needless to say, not part of the conservation area, though a further narrow tongue of river bank, renowned for its fine views across the water, has been included.

If one makes the pilgrimage eastward along narrow Crane Street towards this obstructed stretch of river bank, one may well wonder about the origin of the diminutive but charming group of white stuccoed almshouses, complete with chapel, which has survived beneath the shadows of the chimneys and still stands facing the river wall. This is Trinity Hospital, founded by Henry Howard in 1613 and still supporting twenty pensioners. Over the centuries Trinity Hospital has undergone many alterations, including the rebuilding of the chapel in 1812, but the basic design is still the original. One of the chapel's greatest surviving treasures is an early sixteenth-century stained glass window.

Trinity Hospital

At this point it is interesting to note that not only have these ancient almshouses survived a twentieth-century effluent but also the fury of the tide. The markings on the river wall opposite record the level reached by three exceptionally high tides, one of which almost destroyed the defences – a factor taken into account when the decision was made to embark on the latest scheme for protecting the estuary.

Busy Romney Road, which one has to cross on moving up Park Row away from the river, was first staked out in 1663 but was not brought into use until 1697. It was a replacement for the old walled and highly inconvenient muddy public highway between Deptford and Woolwich, astride which the Queen's House stood but which now lies buried beneath the colonnades. Unlike the old buried road, renowned for the Sir Walter Raleigh cloak incident, Romney Road has few claims to fame – except for its view of the elegant perfectly proportioned building still known as the Queen's House.

In its beautiful setting just within the park, this double cube-shaped building, renowned for its cool classical simplicity, was designed by Inigo Jones in 1617 for James I's queen, Anne of Denmark. When Anne died two years later, the half completed house was thatched over to protect it from the weather until eventually, in 1635, it was completed for Henrietta Maria, wife of Charles I. Now regarded as probably the finest example of a Palladian building in the country, it forms the central block of the famous National Maritime Museum and attracts a lot of tourist attention, not least from Americans who see in it a blue print of the White House.

As well as the park, with its main gates at the top of Park Row, the conservation area includes the small enclave of Regency terraces along and around Park Vista. Somehow or other these houses have survived the incursions of the 1878 railway extension. As the plates on the vicarage and opposite walls indicate, the prime meridian, marking zero degrees longitude, crosses Park Vista about half way along, some hundred and fifty yards short of the bottom of Maze Hill.

Now notable for its fast moving traffic up the eastern side of the park, Maze Hill is the old route between the river and Blackheath. It first came into existence in the fifteenth century as the price of a licence granted to Duke Humphrey when he decided to close an old road (probably part of Watling Street) that ran too close to his palace for his liking.

The small group of eighteenth-century houses, Nos 111 to 115 Maze Hill, stand where the old Crown Inn once stood – just below the great brick pile, with its conspicuous turrets, known as Vanbrugh Castle. Now in use as a boarding-school, Vanbrugh Castle was the dream child of the architect and dramatist, Sir John Vanbrugh (designer of Blenheim Palace) who built it as his own residence and lived here from 1719 to

1726. According to Pevsner, this was "the first private house ever designed consciously to arouse associations with the Middle Ages".

Several of the residential roads, with their stately Victorian and Edwardian villas leading off Maze Hill immediately to the east, are also included in the Greenwich Park conservation area. Various domestic structures of the Roman period were uncovered at the time some of these villas were built though the big discovery confirming the early existence of a Roman settlement came more recently, in 1965, during the laying of a new gas main down through the park.

This work revealed a missing stretch of Watling Street, thereby establishing the route of the old Roman road across the park's north-eastern corner to the east of One Tree Hill where the gradient is easy. It is now hoped that one day another mystery, that of the strangely shaped mounds in the vicinity of the Queen's House, will also be cleared up and more information come to light to explain the elaborate system of inter-communicating passages that lie forty feet or so beneath the turf.

The once private royal park laid out by Le Nôtre was first opened to the public about 1705 after a decision to admit friends of the seamen patients to the hospital grounds – a concession which soon turned it into a major attraction for Londoners on holiday and paved the way for the arrival of the fair. With the fair came the popular and reputedly bawdy sport known as "tumbling down" Observatory Hill which outraged Greenwich residents so much that they finally, in 1857, managed to get the fair suppressed.

A more permanent environmental blotch from which Greenwich Park narrowly escaped in the mid-eighteenth century was a pseudo-classical viaduct. Proponents of the railway extension wanted to erect the proposed viaduct in front of the Queen's House and it was only after a long and bitter struggle that the opposition lobby succeeded in getting the project annulled and a vibration-proof underground tunnel built instead. The effect which the original plan would have had on today's beautifully landscaped park, with its wooded areas, deer reserve, lake and flower gardens, is now fortunately only a matter for the imagination!

These days Greenwich Park attracts not only tourists from all over the world but also archaeologists interested in the ancient burial ground, the unexplained mounds and the site known as The Villa where Roman remains were first uncovered in 1902.

The angular red brick silhouette of the old Royal Observatory which, with its familiar turrets and domes, guides one up the hill via almost any path to the ancient promontory near the middle of the park, stands on the site of the old Greenwich Castle. Descriptions of this well-known landmark, with its superb views over London, vary from "the elegant little observatory" to "that quaint old pile".

The oldest of the present group of buildings is Flamsteed House, named after the first Astronomer Royal in 1675 and the home of his successors right up to 1948. Traditionally Flamsteed House, or the 'Octagon Room' as it is often called, is believed to have been designed by Wren, though some people now attribute it to Edward Strong. Certainly it was the brain child of Charles II who gave just over £500 (raised from the sale of decayed gun powder!) for its construction "in order to the finding out of the longitude of places and for perfecting navigation and astronomy" – a project which in those days was of paramount and urgent importance for the safety of mariners. Whoever was responsible for its design, it seems that this familiar building was erected in haste on an economy budget, using the actual foundations of the old watch-tower (built two centuries earlier by Duke Humphrey) and with second-hand bricks taken from an old fort at Tilbury. The huge red time ball which stands on its roof and drops daily at 1 pm was added in 1833.

The other buildings in the museum group, including the mid-eighteenth-century Meridian Building whose familiar metal strip divides the world into two hemispheres, east and west, had less colourful beginnings. Historically, however, all made their own valuable contributions, first to navigation and then to astronomy. The onion dome of the Great Equatorial Building is a modern version of the onion dome built in 1893 but destroyed by enemy action during the Second World War. To mark the tercentenary of the old observatory and the return of cleaner air to London, the giant 28-inch refractor telescope, which was transferred after the war to Herstmonceux in Sussex, was brought back and, in June 1975, installed in the new dome where it is now used both for research and for teaching purposes.

The monument standing close by on the hilltop is a reminder of James Wolfe's connections with Greenwich. It was presented in 1930 by the Canadian people.

The southern boundary of both park and conservation area is formed by Charlton Way, the main road that separates Greenwich from Blackheath and provides a double-gated entrance through which motor traffic can pass down through the park to King William Walk.

It was in King William Walk (formerly called King Street) that the famous Greenwich Academy started by Thomas Weston, Assistant Astronomer Royal to Flamsteed, stood until it moved in 1782 to a mansion (demolished in 1830 to form Burney Street) at the foot of Croom's Hill. Weston's school was set up to teach reading, writing and navigation to the sons of seamen – a task in which presumably it succeeded judging by the fact that several of its pupils became admirals. It has been said that by Nelson's day, half the flag officers in the fleet received their education at this school.

Standing on its corner between King William Walk and Romney Road, the Dreadnought Seamen's Hospital (originally part of the Royal Hospital) was rebuilt in 1811 after a fire had destroyed the original building of 1763.

As its statue indicates, King William Walk was re-named after William IV, but it was badly damaged during the Second World War and its reconstruction is seen as leaving much to be desired. Nevertheless few would admit to passing down this old street without some sense of exhilaration at the sudden spectacle of the hundred-year-old tea clipper, *Cutty Sark*, standing in full view at the end. What more fitting final touch could there be to the Greenwich splendour?

(ii) WEST GREENWICH
Where the Greenwich Park conservation area ends, West Greenwich begins, taking in part of the old town as well as the delightful network of miniature streets, with their rows of Regency houses on the hillside west of Croom's Hill.

The old town includes the narrow streets and alleyways leading off King William Walk into Greenwich Church Street and Greenwich High Road – the central area now so heavily overladen with traffic. It was here, at the dog-leg bend into Croom's Hill, that the town well once stood. In fact, during the past twenty years, several wells have been uncovered in Stockwell Street, one of them lined with Roman masonry. The latest discovery occurred just outside Greenwich Theatre in March 1970 shortly after Princess Alexandra had attended a

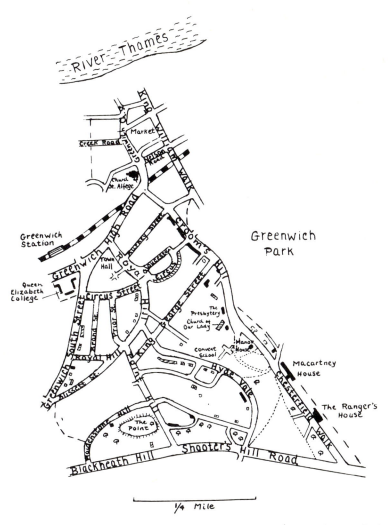

performance there. A sudden subsidence in the road revealed
not only the casing of a large well but also a tunnel leading out
of it in a north-easterly direction.

Stockwell Street and Greenwich High Road (formerly
London Road) owe their present dismal appearance to a
series of unfortunate circumstances. First they were the
victims of serious war damage, then of planning blight and,

finally, in the 1960-70 period, of what one historian has described as irreparable destruction under a redevelopment scheme when "in two disastrous weeks a thousand years of Greenwich's habit of life were torn down and carted away as rubble". However the proposed redevelopment, including the construction of a motorway between a council development on the adjacent four-acre site and Thamesmead on the Woolwich marshes, has not yet materialised and some people think it may still be possible to recapture something of the spirit of this ancient place.

In 1840 a multiplicity of shops and stables was crowded into Stockwell Street but, apart from that, the old town was little touched by the Victorian building boom. Most of the replanning had already been done, around 1825, by Joseph Kay, the architect made responsible for the later work of the Royal Hospital.

St Alfege Church, conspicuous on its corner site between Creek Road and Greenwich High Road, was built much earlier. As one of "50 new churches" provided for in an Act passed during the reign of Queen Anne, it was erected on the site of an eleventh-century church badly damaged in 1710 when the roof fell in, shattering the monuments and destroying much of the fabric. Although remodelled in 1810, the present spacious and solid looking church in Portland stone was built by Nicholas Hawksmoor – its tower was separately designed by John James – and it was consecrated in 1718. Like its predecessor, it was named after St Alfege, the Saxon Archbishop of Canterbury who was kidnapped from his cathedral by the invading Danes, imprisoned at Greenwich and finally, after an abortive rescue attempt, felled to the ground on this particular spot by an infuriated Dane using a large bone, traditionally believed to have been the skull of an ox.

Greenwich Church Street still follows almost exactly the line of the ancient street that ran from the church down to the river. Although long since modernised and converted into shops, Nos 15 to 21, with their narrow façades and tall pitched roofs, are survivors of that period.

The West Greenwich conservation area extends along Greenwich High Road almost as far as the railway station, thereby including the almshouses known as Queen Elizabeth College that stands well back from the street on the north side. Built by the historian William Lambarde in about 1574 and with a foundation based on a modest charity – modest in the sense that there was a long list of benefactions from local people rather than a few large ones from aristocratic sources – this college is regarded as the first of its kind since the Reformation.

As a town dominated by the river, Greenwich was populated for centuries by people connected with ships. It was for them that the speculators of Regency times set about building houses on the hillside west of Croom's Hill to the south of Shooter's Hill Road and it is this area, with Greenwich South Street serving as the western boundary, that constitutes the remaining part of the conservation area.

One can walk up through the middle of it via Royal Hill and Point Hill. Until about 1812 when a speculator called Robert Royal bought the market-garden land on which it is built, Royal Hill was called Gang Lane – a legacy from the Danish occupation of 1012. Robert Royal transformed the area into a flourishing Georgian neighbourhood and was probably directly responsible for Nos 65 to 87 Royal Hill and Nos 3 to 25 King George Street.

The small trim cottage terraces of Prior, Brand and King George Streets were probably intended for the families of skilled hands, while the grander double-fronted houses of Gloucester Circus, usually attributed to a speculator called Launcelot Loat, were no doubt built with the mates, shipwrights and shipping clerks in mind. Nos 21 to 42 Gloucester Circus, built about 1791, are of special interest because they are the work of Michael Searles, the architect who designed 'The Paragon' at nearby Blackheath.

For general architectural interest, however, no road in West Greenwich can compete with Croom's Hill. This steep and narrow lane, with Greenwich Park on its eastern flank, is renowned not only for its magnificent Georgian houses but also for several earlier ones, including Nos 16 and 18 at the bottom of the hill which date back to 1656. Attractive No 34 a little higher up has an 1810 addition at the back but most of it was built in the reign of Charles II. One of its early occupants was a certain Nicholas Wizzall who died in 1720 leaving the poor of Greenwich with a legacy of £4 a year for ever and his wife with "the use of" his silver teapot!

Clearly the early residents of West Greenwich were not without their whims and fancies. Higher up the road the small square gazebo (repaired in 1955) that stands right up to the road on an elevated foundation was built in 1672 for Sir William Hooker, Lord Mayor of London. Hooker was a rich and well-known local character who had established himself in Greenwich at the time of the plague. Like many of his contemporaries, he was encouraged by the absence of the royal overlord, Charles II, to join in the scramble for some of the 'waste land' at the top of the hill – land wedged in between the road and a stretch of the wall which James I had erected around the park in 1619. It was here that Hooker built his so-called 'waste villas', some of which still survive today.

As one walks up the hill, the next building of historical interest after the gazebo is the two-storeyed house with the distinctive gables and brick pilasters which stands just below the Roman Catholic church. Known as 'The Presbytery' (No 66 Croom's Hill), this is regarded architecturally as the most mysterious house put up in Greenwich during the first half of the seventeenth century. It was built as a speculation about 1630 by William Smith, hereditary Sergeant-at-Arms to the King, on land once owned by the great Swanne House. Because of its Dutch appearance it has been linked with the Dutch House at Kew, with Swakeleys in Middlesex and with a house at West Horsley in Surrey, all of which were built about the same time. With its various alterations and additions, it now belongs to the Roman Catholic church and is occupied by priests.

If one follows the path up the steep incline just above the church so as to get a view of the terraced spur of open land to the west, it is interesting to see that there is still only one residential road in sight. Distant Hyde Vale, winding its way up towards Shooter's Hill Road, was developed with detached houses at its upper end early in the nineteenth century.

As for the vantage point itself, this elevated plot of land, with its little enclave of windswept cottages and old manor-house, was originally licensed by James I for the erection of farm buildings. It was not until 1695 that the beautiful two-storeyed house in dark red brick, which still stands close to the path at the point before it begins to drop down again into Croom's Hill, was built for the London merchant, Sir Robert Robinson. In style, the manor house is said to be reminiscent of several City halls built after the Fire of London. Among its prize possessions is some exceptionally fine wood carving presented by both porches, back and front.

The big house on the opposite side of Croom's Hill, known

The Manor House

as Park Hall, was once the home of Sir James Thornhill who
worked for nineteen years on the decorations for the Painted
Hall, while Hillside, now owned by the local authority but
much neglected, was the most northerly of Sir William
Hooker's 'waste villas'.

The pleasant twisting house in amber brick called
Macartney House belongs to the late seventeenth and mid-
eighteenth century, with later additions by Sir John Soane. It
was once the property of Major-General Wolfe and the
occasional residence of his famous son James who conquered
Quebec in 1759 and who was subsequently buried at St
Alfege's. For a time the house was occupied by a well-known
Greenwich speculator called Snape whom the diarist John

Evelyn described as "a man full of projects", and later by Lord Lyttleton.

The White House was the last of Sir William Hooker's 'waste villas' to be built and it was here that Elizabeth Lawson lived – the girl whom James Wolfe is said to have courted unsuccessfully for four unhappy years.

Chesterfield Walk, as this upper end of Croom's Hill is called, takes its name from Philip, Earl of Chesterfield, one-time owner of the two-storeyed mansion in brown brick that stands so prominently behind its fine wrought iron gates at the top of the hill and is now known as the Ranger's House.

The Ranger's House

The Ranger's House was begun in 1688 and the gallery added in 1748, followed by the two bowed wings in 1749. It has had various names, including Chesterfield House, and only acquired its present name after it was bought by the Crown for use as the official residence of the Ranger of Greenwich Park. George III's niece, Sophie Matilda, who lived here in 1815, held this office. In 1900 the property was acquired by the county council and now, partly as a result of action taken by the GLC's Historic Buildings Division, it is used to house the Suffolk Art Collection.

The open corner site between the Ranger's House and Shooter's Hill Road, sometimes known as Montague Corner, takes its name from Montague House that once stood here – a house leased in 1801, in addition to the Ranger's House next door, by the Prince Regent's estranged wife, Caroline, but later pulled down by the Prince in an effort to exorcise her memory!

Shooter's Hill Road, with its roaring traffic and view over the open spaces of the adjoining conservation areas of Blackheath, forms the southern boundary of the West Greenwich conservation area. Thus all that remains are the grassy triangles of common land that stretch westward as far as Point Hill.

The so-called Point Caverns now lie in dark and sinister obscurity beneath this spur of high land, their origins still undetermined with any certainty, though the general theory is that they were constructed during the struggle between the Saxons and the Danes. The largest cavern is said to be about 150 feet long, with several smaller chambers joined to it by passages, all hacked out of the chalk by men using antlers as tools. A Celtic carving of a devil god was found at one entrance and a well at the farthest end, but neither really solved the mystery.

When the largest cavern, often known as the Blackheath Cavern, was accidentally rediscovered in 1780, it produced a fresh crop of excited speculation – so excited, it seems, that genuine historic inquiry quickly degenerated into "riotous and bawdy entertainment". Finally, after the candles had been fed with asafoetida (resinous gum smelling of garlic) and then put out, the cavern was closed.

Today all one can see of West Greenwich's buried past here on the hilltop is an inconspicuous entrance known as the conduit head at the corner of West Grove and Hyde Vale. As the stone inscription in the wall simply states, the conduit head was built in 1740 as part of the water supply for the Royal Hospital for Seamen – a fitting epitaph perhaps for the whole of this historic area which owes so much of its development and present-day interest to the men who fought Britain's battles at sea.

6

Hampstead Village

Keats' House

If asked to name the favourite haunt of some nineteenth-century literary giant, the territory which now forms Hampstead village conservation area would probably be as good a bet as any. After all, what more agreeable habitat could an aesthetically minded person hope to find than that provided by the steep twisting pathways, charming alleyways and backwaters carved out of the southern slopes of one of the capital's highest hills.

However it is worth remembering that it was not the novelists, poets and artists who first set this old Saxon hamlet of Ham-stede (meaning homestead or farm), that had grown out of a clearing in the vast Middlesex forest, on the road to fame. That distinction belongs to an earlier group of people of

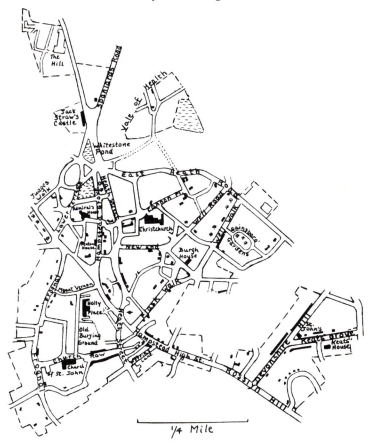

1/4 Mile

distinctly more mundane calling – namely to a colony of
sixteenth-century washer-women who established themselves
here in order to avail themselves of an apparently unlimited
supply of their most valuable commodity – pure water.

Since time immemorial, Hampstead's numerous springs
had supplied the nearby ponds and several of London's rivers
but until now this domestic potential had been neither
recognised nor exploited. The oversight however was quickly
rectified and, in its new-found role, Hampstead became
almost a household word. Many of London's most important
people were among the customers and even royalty, it is said,
sent it their washing!

The next turning point in Hampstead's history was again due to the springs. Early in the eighteenth century a resident physician called Gibbons published a list of various 'cures' effected by drinking the water and, in doing so, wittingly or unwittingly transformed the old village almost overnight into "a resort of the wealthy, the idle and the sickly", with the usual supporting services such as "houses of entertainment and dissipation".

This sudden popularity, accentuated by the appearance of large country mansions built for rich merchants and professional men, with an attendant influx of lesser mortals, inevitably spelt the end of the old village and led the way to the succession of ownerships that followed.

In Saxon times, King Ethelred had given the manor to the Abbey of Westminster, who held it until forced to surrender to Henry VIII in 1539. However the period of royal ownership was brief. After twelve years, Henry's successor, Edward VI, gave it to a certain Sir Thomas Wroth in whose family it remained until 1620 when it was sold to Sir Baptist Hicks, afterwards Lord Camden. Through Lord Camden it eventually passed to the Gainsborough family but the Gainsboroughs sold out in 1707 and there followed a long succession of private owners until, in 1900, the village became officially part of Greater London.

If one decides to surface from Hampstead's 192-feet deep underground station (the deepest in London and once a popular Second World War refuge against air-raids), the traffic hazards of Heath Street have to be faced before reaching the comparative calm of Holly Hill on the opposite side of the road, but most people agree that the reward is worth it.

Running roughly north and south, Heath Street virtually bisects the conservation area. It was almost entirely rebuilt in 1887-94, whereas the High Street which joins it at this busy junction was left more or less to its own devices until given a successful face-lift under a Civic Trust scheme in 1962. These were the old high roads that passed through the original village.

The steep and narrow thoroughfare known as Holly Hill was originally the northern section of the High Street and was probably part of a single road linking Hendon to London. It may be a thousand years old or more. With its quaint miniature side streets and unexpected flights of steps, it is believed that the whole of the Holly Hill area may once have been covered with holly trees – a pleasant scene to imagine as one climbs the shady pedestrian pathways.

With so many inviting roads or lanes ahead, the choice of a route to the celebrated Heath may present something of a dilemma. However one can reserve the upper reaches of the hillside for later exploration and turn off to the west along Mount Vernon Lane at the top of Holly Hill, just short of the Medical Council Research Laboratories. Alas, this complex of large red-brick laboratories is now seen as something of an architectural blotch on the much prized landscape.

The road with the curious name of Frognal that runs roughly north and south at the end of Mount Vernon Lane lies just within the eastern boundary of the conservation area. Although the earliest settlement in 'Ham-stede' is thought to have been near the junction of Frognal with Frognal Lane lower down – a manor-house was later built here – the origin of the name is still a matter for conjecture. One popular theory is that the manor-house came to be known as Frogen Hall – 'frogen' being the Saxon for frogs – on account of three nearby ponds!

As an alternative to taking the Frognal route down towards Church Row where the old tollgate once stood, one can turn southward halfway along Mount Vernon Lane and walk down that delightful lane, Holly Walk, with its unusual T-shaped terrace (listed property) on the east side, containing St Mary's Church in the middle. Built in 1816, St Mary's is one of London's earliest Roman Catholic churches. The three cul-de-sacs, including Benham's Place (1813), also made their appearances early in the nineteenth century, and so did the old burying ground near the bottom of the hill. The burying ground was purchased in 1811 when it was realised that St John's churchyard, diagonally opposite in Church Row, was becoming overcrowded.

Despite its plain brick structure, the eighteenth-century parish church of St John is not without its picturesque touches and peculiarities. Because the tower is at the east instead of at the west end and there is an entrance beneath it looking out along Church Row in the direction of Heath Street, St John's has a reputation for looking like "a church turned round"

Until the 1880s this church on a hill – the land continues to fall steeply away from it both to the south and to the west – stood in the middle of a quiet precinct and was approached

Church of St John, Downshire Hill

only by way of small alleys and Little Church Row.
Apparently its medieval predecessor, a church of stone and
timber with a wooden tower, had been built not for the benefit
of the villagers but for the monks of Westminster in their
abbey three hundred and fifty feet lower down, the purpose
being to provide these holy men with a church to which they
could "lift their eyes".

Both terraces at the Heath Street end of Church Row
preceded the present church, the one on the north side being
the older. It is believed that some of the houses here, notably
No 5 with its white-painted weather-boarded first and second
floors jutting out over the pavement, date back to before 1700.
Those on the south side, including No 26 once occupied by

George Gilbert Scott and more recently by the actress Moira Shearer and her husband Ludovic Kennedy, were mostly built by speculators in the early part of the eighteenth century.

The three narrow lanes, including Perrin's Court still with its overhead archway, that lead through into Hampstead High Street from the lower end of Heath Street (extended in 1912) are all old. Perrin's Lane, is probably one of the oldest paths in Hampstead for it used to link the original settlement in Frognal with the old high road.

The conservation area takes in the whole length of the High Street but, as the gradient steepens and it becomes Rosslyn Hill, there is a short stretch of non-designated territory before one reaches the Downshire Hill – Keats Grove area, well known for its associations with the youthful poet and the house in which he lived.

The road called Downshire Hill, with its gentle slope towards the lower part of the heath, has been described as one of the prettiest roads in Hampstead and is well known for its simple dignified New England building set at an angle of about thirty degrees at the corner of Keats Grove. Now known as St John's Church, Downshire Hill, to distinguish it from the parish church, the building was originally designed as a chapel-of-ease.

Keats' House, lower down Keats Grove, was reopened to the public on 2nd September, 1975, after a period of restoration. Originally called Wentworth Place, it was built in 1815 as two dwellings, one of which was occupied by Keats and his friend Charles Brown. Here it was that the poet spent the last three years of his life, from 1818 to 1820, composing some of his greatest poetry and falling in love with Fanny Brawne, daughter of a neighbouring family.

This graceful compact house was rescued from destruction many years ago by the Pilgrim's Trust, the Keats-Shelley Association of America and by public subscription, but by 1974 it was in urgent need of restoration and was closed for twelve months whilst the work was carried out by Camden Borough Council at a cost of £70,000 under the direction of the consultant architect, Mr John Brandon-Jones, with assistance from the Victoria and Albert Museum. As far as is humanly possible, the house now looks much as it did when Keats lived there.

After walking back along the High Street as far as Flask Walk near the underground station, one can begin to explore

Perrin's Court

the extensive network of roads and lanes that lie between upper Heath Street and the conservation area's eastern boundary, East Heath Road. With its shops and inn at one end, its small alleyways and its row of old-fashioned cottages leading to the remnants of a village green at the other, Flask Walk is still almost a village in itself. Until 1911, when the council pulled it down, a picturesque archway-entrance similar to the one which still exists in Perrin's Court stood at the Heath Street entrance, no doubt adding to the air of self containment.

Before 1873, when it was rebuilt, the Flask Tavern was known as the Lower Flask Inn or the Thatch'd House. This was where Hampstead's celebrated medicated water used to be bottled ready for collection each day by carrier's wagon for distribution all over London. At threepence (old currency) a flask – flasks to be returned daily – the water was in great demand, especially by sufferers from those early eighteenth century complaints attributed to dissipation and idleness.

In those days Flask Walk also had a reputation for attracting the more raffish elements of society and appears to have been the scene of much bawdy entertainment, especially when the annual fairs were in progress on the village green, prior to their suppression in 1821.

All that now remains of the village green is the pleasant triangular space (rather quaintly overlooked since the last century by the council's wash-houses) at the end of this fascinating thoroughfare. It was here that the stocks stood on the site now occupied by telephone kiosks, with the watchman's hut and two overnight cells, mainly for use by people who were 'uncivil' to the parson, close by.

No 48 Flask Walk is listed partly on account of its handsome Regency door, though it is now thought that the door was acquired from a more important house some distance away. The owner believes the little house was built as a pair of railway cottages.

The name given to the continuation road, Well Walk, speaks for itself. During the watering-place era, this was the promenade that led to the assembly room and pump room, jointly known as the long room. Even today when all that remains of the buildings and well is a trickle of spring water from a stone fountain – the diminished flow is due to the deep drains and railway tunnel – it is not difficult to imagine the bath chairs and donkeys that used to ply their way laboriously back and forth in the shade of the elm trees.

Increasing complaints about riotous assemblies and bad debts brought those days to an end but, even after the spa premises had been closed and the land sold for redevelopment as a chapel, people continued to be attracted by the residential merits of this part of Hampstead, just as they were to the higher slopes. In fact, judging by the number of blue plaques, its appeal to those destined to achieve fame of one kind or another was just as great.

Even the ordinary, unmarked and somewhat inconvenient looking end-terrace house, No 14, at the beginning of Well Walk had its celebrated tenant shortly after the turn of the present century in the person of Marie Stopes. After her first disastrous marriage, the scientist-author lived here for several years, presumably contemplating the books that were to become best sellers.

Architecturally of course it is Burgh House on the opposite (north) side of the road that attracts the attention at the 'village green' end of Well Walk. Standing well back on its plot of high ground at the corner of New End Square, this attractive red brick house was built in 1702. In its affluent days its picture was included in a Wedgwood dinner service commissioned by the Empress of Russia, but such glory did not last and, in later years, Burgh House was subjected to a variety of indignities, including a spell of duty as the Middlesex Militia barracks. Although given a new lease of life in modern times, the intrusion of the Wells House council flats complex which partially obscures it from view now seems an irreversible fact of life.

The Wells House flats are so named because they stand on the site of Hampstead's second long room – a building which eventually came to be occupied as a private residence by the poet John Masefield. Despite protests from preservationists, Weatherall House, as it came to be known, was demolished in 1948.

The Wells Tavern at the corner of Well Walk and Christchurch Hill is a replacement pub for the original inn of the same name, once one of Hampstead's oldest houses of entertainment, while the oval plantation and surrounding houses called Gainsborough Gardens that lie behind it occupy the site of the extensive pleasure gardens of the old spa.

The three-storeyed terrace house, No 40, at this far end of Well Walk, recognisable by the galaxy of drain pipes at the front, was the first real home of John Constable (1770-1837). At least it was the first house in which he and his large family were able to enjoy the comforts of their own furniture. Previously they had spent a year in Downshire Hill and before that had lived for several years in furnished cottage accommodation in Lower Terrace. When they arrived here in Well Walk in 1827, it is said that one of the painter's greatest thrills was the view from the drawing-room at the back of the house – a view right over London. Unfortunately his happiness was short-lived for, in 1828, soon after the birth of his seventh child, his wife Maria died of pulmonary tuberculosis.

Like several other parts of Hampstead, Well Walk is also associated with John Keats (1795-1821). In the days before he moved to Downshire Hill, the young poet and his two brothers were lodgers at the postman's house (now demolished) next door to the Wells Tavern and it is said that his favourite seat, as identified in several old prints, stood at the end of the walk on the side of the elms. From here Keats must have had a splendid view of the heath stretching away to the north and east beyond the adjacent road known as East Heath Road that now forms the boundary of this north-eastern part of the conservation area.

As East Heath Road winds its way up the hill as far as Whitestone Pond, there is still more evidence of the lure which Hampstead had for the writing community. The three-storeyed semi-detached Victorian villa, No 17 East Heath Road, situated on one of the road's most hazardous bends, is where Katherine Mansfield (1883-1923) chose to live with her husband, the critic John Middleton Murry.

The isolated little colony in the hollow known as the Vale of Health, approached via the country-looking lane off to the north opposite Squire's Lane, is a separate part of the conservation area. Standing beside one of Hampstead's largest ponds and with the heath all around it, its name is based on the belief that it escaped the ravages of the plague of 1665.

In a house typical of this colony of small sea-side type dwellings, namely No 1 Byron Villas, lived the poet and novelist, D.H. Lawrence (1883-1930) during the year 1915. The other main literary association is with the Indian poet Tagore who lived in one of the villas on the heath near the centre.

Back in the boisterous wind of East Heath Road, one is close to Hampstead's highest point. The large block of flats (Bell Moor) at the top stands 437 feet above sea level. This means that it is higher than St Paul's cross. J. Barratt, historian of Hampstead, lived here from 1877 to 1914 in the house that previously stood on the site.

Although Whitestone Pond provides some degree of refuge, one may not feel that the junction of Heath Street and Spaniards Road, where the traffic swirls around one from almost every direction, is the ideal place to pause and take one's bearings. However this area, together with 'Jack Straw's Castle' and the small triangle of land just beyond it, forms the northern apex of the conservation area.

The 1962 version of 'Jack Straw's Castle' replaced the old inn which used to be one of Dickens' favourite haunts – an inn first mentioned in 1713 but badly damaged during the Second World War. The inclusion of the word 'castle' in the name arose from the legend that there was once a prehistoric encampment on the site. However there appears to be no archaeological evidence to support the legend. As for Jack Straw, he was one of the leaders of the Peasants' Revolt of 1381, a lieutenant of Wat Tyler, who is said to have mustered his forces on this spot. With the heath stretching out on almost every side, the area also has plenty of associations with highwaymen, including Dick Turpin.

From Whitestone Pond it is possible to follow the rough path around the Hawthorne Nursing Home to join Judges Walk. Tradition has it that this wider path with the spectacular view was where the judges came to take refuge during the plague. Branch Hill and the continuation road Frognal, running southward, are just within the western boundary of the conservation area.

The more devious and more interesting alternative route down the hill via Lower Terrace, Admiral's Walk and Hampstead Grove takes one past Netley Cottage. Standing behind the grassy bank in Lower Terrace, it seems that this secluded little house once provided a hiding place for Dick Turpin and his confederates. The clue, only recently discovered, is a grille in an old outside wall leading to a cavity with seating accommodation for several men, followed by a passageway into the rear of Admiral's House in the adjacent thoroughfare of Admiral's Walk.

The terrace lower down the hill includes the small cottage,

No 2 Lower Terrace, which Constable rented furnished in 1821. Cramped though he and his ever-growing family must have been, it was here that the painter produced some of his finest cloudscapes.

It is thought that the recently painted white-walled house with the lime-green shutters called Grove Lodge on the middle bend of Admiral's Walk may once have been a farm-house. Early this century however it became the home of John Galsworthy. He lived here from 1918 to 1933, the period during which he completed *The Forsyte Saga*. Originally he rented the house for only three years but is said to have become so attached to the place that he stayed on until his death in 1933 at the age of sixty-five.

The much larger Queen Anne house joined to Grove Lodge at right angles acquired its name, Admiral's House, from the fact that it was once the home of the eccentric Admiral Matthew Barton (1715-95). Hence the extra roof constructed like the deck of a ship and complete with a couple of cannons. Early in the morning and dressed in full uniform, the Admiral used to stand on his 'deck', with its magnificent view over London, and fire his cannons to celebrate past naval victories. A later occupant of the house – from 1856 to 1864 – was Sir George Gilbert Scott, champion of the Gothic Revival style of architecture and designer of St Pancras Station.

The hum of traffic one hears from over the roof tops of Mount Square at the end of Admiral's Walk comes from Heath Street down below. Among the group of fine eighteenth-century houses here in Hampstead Grove are numbers 26 and 28. George du Maurier lived at No 28 from 1874 to 1895.

But it is to Fenton House, a little lower down on the west side of Hampstead Grove, that the chief honours go. This is considered one of Hampstead's earliest, largest and architecturally one of its best houses. Built in 1693, Fenton House is now National Trust property, housing a collection of paintings, porcelain and keyboard instruments, including the Benton-Fletcher collection, and is open daily to the public except on Mondays and Tuesdays.

The four houses facing Holly Bush Hill farther down the hill were built around 1730 and all are listed. The one on the corner is where the painter George Romney (1734-1802) once lived, and what a view he must have had from those upper windows!

If one chooses to descend into Heath Street via any of the

steep little offshoots from Holly Bush Hill instead of **via Holly Hill**, the group of small higgledy-piggledy shops at the bottom comes as a reminder of what this main thoroughfare probably once looked like.

Holly Bush Steps

The old and narrow street on the opposite side of Heath Street has long been noted for its elm trees and was named accordingly. The north side of Elm Row was developed as a speculation about 1720 and in the late nineteenth-century Sir Henry Cole, founder of the Kensington Museum and originator of the Christmas card custom, occupied No 3 of the stately main terrace.

As Elm Row turns itself through a right angle into Hampstead Square, with its own important complement of early eighteenth-century houses, it is interesting to recall that this was once a regular place for performances by strolling players, especially during the early nineteenth century. Christchurch on the corner site was consecrated in 1852 and has a gallery designed by George Gilbert Scott.

If one takes advantage of Hampstead's natural contours which enable one to meander, it is pleasant to follow the Christchurch Passage – New End – Streatley Place route back towards the underground station at the bottom of the hill. For here there is time to remember, before the roar of modern traffic re-envelops one, how the potentialities and advantages of an old Saxon village came to be recognised and how, in the course of time, they turned it into something much more than just a luxurious suburb.

7

Hanwell – Churchfields and Village Green

The Hermitage

The yellow brick Victorian station of Hanwell, now under threat of demolition, lies just within the eastern boundary of the scenic and exhilarating Churchfields conservation area. Since this is an area dominated by the famous Wharncliffe Viaduct, it means that, within minutes of leaving the station, one has a fine close-up view of the majestic structure designed by the great engineer Brunel and named after the chairman of the parliamentary committee responsible for it.

The original station stood just above the point where the road passes under one of the viaduct's eight superb elliptical arches but, apart from that, this section of the line seems to have changed very little since the Great Western Railway

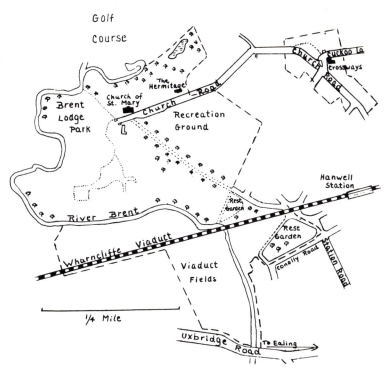

opened to traffic in 1838. The viaduct spans a seven-hundred foot stretch of the deep broad valley scooped out over the ages by the winding River Brent, and it is easy to understand why Queen Victoria, whenever she travelled over it, used to ask that the driver of the train should slow down so that she could admire the view.

Inevitably the view today is different from that seen by Queen Victoria and it is doubtful whether anyone would now want to stop a train in order to look southward at the chaos which is Uxbridge Road. But the scene on the north side has proved almost as resilient to change as the viaduct itself. Here, where the old village of Hanwell stands at the top of the hill, the spire of the early Victorian church still pierces the wooded skyline and green fields still rise up towards it.

To the conservation minded, there may be some satisfaction in the knowledge that these undulating acres, bounded on the north and west by the winding river and including Brent

The Wharncliffe Viaduct

Lodge Park, are now public land intended to be preserved for posterity. Nowadays some of the land is used for formal recreational purposes and two wooded dells, with their sheltering clusters of fine old trees, have been set aside as 'rest gardens', but most of the river bank itself has been purposely left in its natural state.

If one takes the long diagonal path across the recreation ground leading to the church, one may partly guess at the story of Hanwell. A ridge of land rising steeply upward from the river, as this does, was exactly what early settlers are known to have looked for, so there was no real surprise when, during the past century, hundreds of flint implements, portions of clay vases and other objects of the Stone and Bronze Ages were discovered here. There is also evidence that, at a later stage in history, the tribe of Ancient Britons known as the Catavellauni lived in the area.

The name Hanwell (spelt Hanewelle in a document of 957 and again in the Domesday Book) is thought to be derived from the Anglo-Saxon word 'han', meaning a boundary stone, and 'well', meaning a spring or fresh water.

For years the so-called Hanwell Stone, which weighs over a ton, stood in the garden of the old rectory – a reputedly plain house covered with grape vine next to the church. The stone was only removed to Elthorne Park (where it is now) when the old house was demolished earlier this century to make way for flats and maisonettes. If it is the great glacial boulder it is believed to be, its presence in Hanwell could mean that this part of Middlesex was the final point of the Ice Age. According to the Middlesex historian Sir Montagu Sharpe, the Hanwell Stone was certainly here at the time of the

Romans and was probably used by them as a boundary or measuring stone.

As for the 'well', such a one still exists close by in the wooded area behind the Spring Court flats. Before the flats were built, the well belonged to a large eighteenth-century house called 'The Spring' which stood on the site.

One of Hanwell's connections with the Anglo-Saxon period concerns St Dunstan. According to a surviving manuscript of 959, St Dunstan accepted the Hanwell lands as security against a loan of thirty pounds of silver to the lord of the manor, Alfwyn, who wanted to go on a pilgrimage to Rome. On his return, Alfwyn was unable to repay the debt but was nevertheless allowed to remain in possession of the estate throughout his lifetime and only later was the manor handed over to the monastery of St Peter at Westminster.

From the conservation point of view, one soon realises how fortunate the north-western corner of Hanwell is in being a dead end, with nothing beyond the church except the attractive wooden entrance into Brent Lodge Park. This means that, for the motorist, there are only two alternatives: to turn back or leave the vehicle in the small car park and become a pedestrian.

Enclosed on three sides by the winding river, Brent Lodge Park is named after a house dating back to at least 1795 which stood roughly where the park kiosk now stands, just beyond the aviary. This old house was surrounded by a cluster of cottages and occupied from 1884 by Sir Montagu Sharpe who moved in after abandoning the main house of the estate, Hanwell Park. Brent Lodge was originally called Brent End because it stood near the western end of the large well-timbered Hanwell Park estate which, in its time, covered virtually the whole of the territory now occupied by the two conservation areas and the developed land in between. Still remembered for its beautiful pointed Gothic windows, Brent Lodge became a temporary home early in the nineteenth century for two of Shelley's children, Ianthe and Charles, who stayed here whilst in the custody of a Dr Thomas Hume. Montagu Sharpe finally sold out to the council in 1930 and the house was then demolished.

Standing adjacent to the entrance into Brent Lodge Park, the present-day church of St Mary, built in the Gothic Revival period with black flints and bricks, with stone dressings, is the fourth Christian church to be built on this site. The earliest of the four, erected possibly on the site of a pagan shrine of the Roman era, is known to have existed in 958. During the twelfth century the primitive Saxon building of King Edgar's time was replaced by a small thatched church about the length of a cricket pitch and this lasted about six hundred years. A picture of this second church hangs in the rector's vestry. But in 1782 the thatched church was in a bad state and was too small for the needs of the village so it too was demolished and a somewhat unattractive plain oblong brick church with cupola, two bells and a clock erected in its place. Sixty years later this building also proved too small and in 1841 the present church was built. It was designed by Sir George Gilbert Scott – the first of his churches and not considered among his best, but nevertheless one which helped to establish his reputation.

Unfortunately nowadays the building has to be kept locked, though it is open for two hours on Sunday afternoons during the summer. It consists of a nave with aisles and clerestory, and a chancel added in 1897. The attractive early Victorian stained glass windows at the east end were transferred to the present position after the chancel was built.

The crypt probably belonged to the Georgian church but, since access is by way of a trap door under the carpet at the west end of the aisle, it is unlikely that one will be invited to visit it. It consists of a narrow passage with bricked up vaults on either side and is of interest because in it Jonas Hanway was buried, at his own request.

Jonas Hanway was the man who, despite much ridicule, introduced the umbrella to London. He had seen umbrellas in use in Paris, notably by the macaronis, and on his return to England persisted in using one for thirty years before they were generally adopted. Obviously an original, this world-wide traveller, writer and philanthropist founded the Marine Society and later became a social reformer, especially on behalf of poor children, including the climbing boys used in those days as chimney sweeps. He used to visit Hanwell regularly to see his relative and friend, the Reverend Sam Glasse, and became much attached to the place. He died in 1786.

Several other notable people lie buried at Hanwell, including Gainsborough's two sisters, whose grave and raised flat memorial stone occupies one of the plots at the front of the churchyard overlooking the main road.

Despite the seclusion of this old cul-de-sac, the late eighteenth-century Gothic-styled Rectory Cottage opposite the church owes its present derelict burnt-out condition to vandalism and to its subsequent abandonment by two successive owners. Perhaps in some respects its sad fate echoes the misfortunes which befell the old charity school building – a building probably known originally as Church House and reportedly repaired by the churchwardens in 1615. That also once stood opposite the church.

Hanwell's charity school was started in 1779 when the trustees of the Hobbayne Charity (a charity dating back to 1484 when a Hanwell man named William Hobbayne left his lands to be used for "godly purposes") decided to use some of the money to pay a master from Brentford to teach twenty-eight children of Hanwell whose parents wanted them to read and write. But in 1799 part of the school was blown down in a hurricane and the schoolmaster and his wife narrowly escaped injury. Although the school was rebuilt in 1805, it was struck by lightning and again burnt out, leaving the children with only the church for a school-room until other accommodation could be provided.

If one leaves the scene of these misfortunes behind and walks up winding Church Road, with its abundance of mature trees on both sides, one can guess at some of the other character changes which Hanwell has undergone, particularly this century. Most of the smaller houses were built as infills between three large eighteenth-century houses (The Spring, Madge Hill and The Grove) which stood their ground until after the Second World War when they were demolished to make way for the existing small groups of flats.

The striking neo-Gothic cottage-style house known as 'The Hermitage', No 8 Church Road, with its thatched roof, white painted walls and ogival doorway, is one of old Hanwell's few surviving properties and is now listed. It was built about 1810.

Higher up on the opposite side of Church Road, just within the village green conservation area, the L-shaped Spring Cottage (No 99 Church Road), white-washed and with Gothic leaded casements, also dates back to the early nineteenth century. It was here that the old post office once stood beside the ancient triangular village green.

Although now shrunken in size, bisected by the road and beset by a motley collection of posts and railings, it is interesting to see that the green still provides an attractive

focal point for the old village and, as such, has given Hanwell
a small additional conservation area.

Standing on the corner of Cuckoo Lane at the entrance to
the Brent Valley Golf Club, the diminutive ivy-clad Lodge
House, with its Gothic-style windows and unusual chimney
stack, is all that remains of the once private estate of The
Grove. The little house was recently renovated by the Hanwell
Preservation Society but the society is well aware of the
marring effect of the corrugated extension and the untidiness
of the adjacent ground.

Although not much is known of its history, the south-facing
house called 'Crossways' which stands sideways on to the
green is undoubtedly the most interesting house in the
vicinity. Formerly it was known as St Vincent's Lodge and the
long squat building, now rendered and pebble-dashed and
with a superimposed archway of classical design around the
doorway, was originally constructed of brick.

The present-day rectory, on the southern corner of the
green, was built between the two world wars on the site of the
old Hanwell Collegiate College – a boarding-school established
about 1820 for boys destined mainly for Sandhurst or the
Indian Service. Some of the 'diaries of work' of these pupils still
survive and provide graphic descriptions of Victorian Hanwell.

Those days have gone and so has part of the old village, yet
many of the forest trees one sees belong to that distant era.
Like the river, they appear hardly to have changed at all.

Oddly enough, the river is more countrified here in Hanwell
than it is farther out from London. By following its delightful
course in a south-westerly direction from the pool in the wood
beside the golf course, all round Brent Lodge Park, one comes
back to the final stretch of unspoilt river bank within the
Churchfields conservation area, set in the dramatic shadow of
the mighty viaduct.

8

Harrow-on-the-Hill

The Old Schools

(i) HARROW SCHOOL

If only because of their commanding positions and
magnificent views it would be difficult to overlook the two
conservation areas that stand on the narrow winding ridge at
the top of Harrow Hill.

The ancient church in their midst stands 405 feet above sea
level on one of the highest points in Middlesex, some two-
hundred feet higher than the surrounding plain. For centuries
its slender spire has been an unmistakable landmark for
miles around and nowadays it has to carry a round-the-clock
lantern for the benefit of aircraft.

With their terraces and stone steps. most of the stolid windswept Victorian buildings at this northern end of the hill,
standing close to but on slightly lower ground than Harrow
Church, belong to Harrow School and it is for this reason that

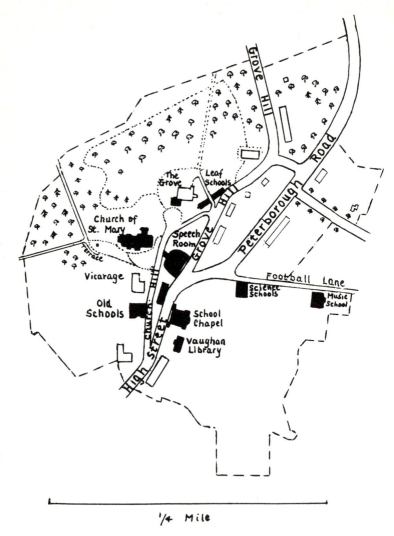

¼ Mile

the conservation area has been designated 'school' to distinguish it from the adjoining 'village' on the southern slopes.

If one starts at Harrow-on-the-Hill underground station just outside the 'school' conservation area and climbs the steep hill by way of Grove Hill – with its precipitous bends, this is an ancient way – it is easy to understand how the original Harrow developed. One of the more popular theories about the derivation of the name is that it came from the Anglo-Saxon word 'hearh', meaning a holy place or tribal sanctuary. Certainly the indications are that the first inhabitants were Saxons who, unlike the Romans, preferred to settle on hilltop sites well above the impenetrable forests below. There is a tradition that before the Saxons were converted to Christianity and long before Lanfranc's Norman church was built, a heathen temple stood here.

Lanfranc came from the great abbey of Le Bec in Normandy at the request of William the Conqueror and was made Archbishop of Canterbury. He was given the Harrow lands previously held by King Harold's brother Leofwine and in 1087 set about building the church which was subsequently consecrated in 1094 by his successor Anselm. Although so far no trace of any earlier Christian church has been found, it is thought highly likely that there was one.

On the site now occupied by The Grove next to the church stood the house of the rector. In medieval times the rector was usually a man of eminence nominated by the Archbishop of Canterbury to supervise the work of the church, including that of the vicar. It is believed that the old vicarage also stood close by, probably on the site of the present vicarage just south of Harrow Church. In addition there was the archbishop's manor house, known to have been used as a convenient resting place between London and the court at Woodstock, but nobody is quite sure where that stood.

One only has to climb the hill in January or February to understand the thinking of John Lyon when he devised one of the statutes for his free grammar school – the school that was to develop into the famous establishment it is today. The boys, he directed, should be kept warm in winter!

John Lyon was a well-to-do yeoman from the nearby hamlet of Preston who, despite all the troubles and dissensions associated with Harrow's determination to remain Catholic at the time of the Reformation, continued to attend the church of St Mary. His plan was to found a school by endowing and reconstituting an older church school which had languished and in 1572 he succeeded in obtaining a charter for the purpose from Elizabeth I.

As the years went by it is reported that John Lyon grew "shorter in breath and longer in memory" as he trudged regularly up the hill to church but his plans for the establishment of "a school house with habitation for master and usher" seem never to have faltered. Naturally his thoughts turned to a site as near as possible to the church he knew so well.

The original endowment was ridiculously small but in his will John Lyon directed that after his death and that of his wife Joan his landed property was to be used for the upkeep of the school – a provision which enabled the west wing of what is now known as the 'Old Schools' to be built about the year 1610, some two years after Joan Lyon's death.

A more controversial statute than the one concerned with keeping the boys warm was John Lyon's direction that girls should be totally excluded. On the other hand, 'foreigners', meaning boys from a distance, could be admitted on terms which allowed the schoolmaster "to take such stipend as he can get". It was this quaint clause which, despite vigorous protests in 1810 from the inhabitants of Harrow, enabled Harrow School to become mainly a fee-paying establishment catering for the sons of wealthy people outside the parish.

Some of the school's large boarding-houses which one passes on the journey up Grove Hill – the conservation area begins at Elmsfield Cottage just above the corner of Tyburn Lane – include 'The Copse' presented by E.E.B. (Edward Ernest Brown), reputedly the greatest of school songsters.

A little higher up, the recently built Leaf Schools incorporate the derelict stables from which R.B. Sheridan's well equipped coach used to sally forth on its regular trips to London. "These form rooms embody the walls of Sheridan's stables" declares the tablet on the wall, and they are in fact Harrow's only remaining memorial to the famous playwright. The house in which he lived in great magnificence (reputedly not on ready money but on expectations) with his lovely, but often lonely wife, in the years up to 1784 was destroyed by fire in 1833. Still known as The Grove, the rebuilt house with its footpath leading up to the church behind the Leaf schools recently underwent major restoration.

The tablet on the art school just above the Leaf Schools was affixed in 1925 and the legend tells its own story: "Near this spot on 27th April, 1646, King Charles I, when fleeing from Oxford with two companions on his way to surrender to the Scottish Army at Southall, rested to take a last look at London, and to water his horses at the Spring which still runs below and has ever since been called King Charles' well". The spring referred to formed a pond and for a long time it was one of Harrow's water supplies. However when Rendalls, the large boarding-house on the opposite side of the road, was built in 1854, the pond was filled in.

The conspicuous semi-circular speech room which backs on to Church Hill was built in 1874 as the school assembly hall and, like most of the school buildings in the High Street, including the war memorial building next to it, it is now on the scheduled list of protected buildings.

The conservation area takes in part of steep and narrow Football Lane which branches off the High Street to the east and thereby includes the science schools, museum and music school.

Back in the High Street it is interesting to note that both the School Chapel (1839) and the Vaughan Library were built by Sir George Gilbert Scott. The library was a memorial to Dr Charles Vaughan, headmaster from 1845 to 1859, and small and modest though it is, it houses a fine collection of old bibles and other treasures as well as some ten thousand books. Its foundation stone was laid in 1861 by Lord Palmerston, an old boy of the school, who appears to have left quite an impression behind him. The story is that, although seventy-seven years of age, Lord Palmerston arrived from London on a white horse, laid the foundation stone in torrents of rain, declined any refreshment and rode straight back to the House of Commons.

The building which stands opposite the Head Master's house on the opposite side of the High Street is 'Druries'. With its terraced garden to front and side, this famous school house was almost entirely rebuilt earlier this century. It was here, on the site of the garden, that the 'Crown and Anchor', otherwise known as the 'Abode of Bliss' because the landlord's name was Bliss, once stood.

For a long time this part of the High Street was an area of derelict buildings. It included a Dame's house, the old post office and the old tuck shop, all of which were pulled down for the High Street improvement earlier this century. This is as far as the 'school' conservation area goes along the High Street but there remains Church Hill on the north-west side, with its most interesting of all the school buildings – the Old Schools or, as it is sometimes known, the 'Fourth Form Room'.

Standing conspicuously at the top of the sets of stone steps, Old Schools is now mainly a show piece, used on ceremonial occasions. The west wing (left facing) is the original school building erected about 1610 and looking much as it did when built. The east wing, which contains the old speech room, is a much later addition carried out in 1820 but in perfect harmony with the rest. The Fourth Form Room still contains its ancient seats and desks and the walls are covered with hundreds of carved names, many of them historically familiar, cut into the oak panelling.

The Bill yard stands on the site of an ancient milling ground and is where the fights of the school used to take place a century ago. It is now used on half holidays for call-over.

As the rising path takes one past the vicarage up to the lych gate into the churchyard, it soon becomes apparent that the church of St Mary has been greatly restored. This is a very different church from that which John Byrkhede, master builder and friend of the Archbishop of Canterbury, altered between the years 1437 and 1467. Byrkhede replaced an Early English nave by the present one of carved oak and rebuilt the aisles and clerestory in Perpendicular style. At the same time a south porch with parvise (a priest's room or chapel) was added and also an upper storey to the tower, followed by the famous spire, making the church larger and more important than ever before. Yet today it is doubtful whether John Lyon or those who went before him (including at least one family of martyrs, the Bellamies, some of whom are buried in the church) would recognise it.

After the decision was taken to restore the church, Sir George Gilbert Scott was appointed to undertake the work and during the years 1846-9 he reconstructed the chancel, added the battlemented parapets and, with the exception of the tower, re-faced the church with flint – changes which have by no means met with universal approval.

One thing which remains as remarkable as ever is the view from the tower. On a clear day Highgate and Hampstead can still be seen in the east and St Paul's, with London all around it, in the south-east.

The terrace just beyond the churchyard is equally well renowned for its view of the countryside west of Harrow – the view which, according to tradition, kept Byron sitting or lying dreaming hour after hour on the flat tomb stone known as the 'Peachey Stone'. John Peachey was an old Harrow resident and his tomb only acquired its ugly iron cage about the turn of the century when it was found necessary to protect it from

Church of St Mary

innumerable Byron souvenir hunters. The other Byron
connection is the grave of his daughter Allegra who lies buried
beneath the church porch.

Famous names remain important at Harrow-on-the-Hill
and in modern times probably none more so than that of one
of the seven prime ministers who spent their schooldays here.
With Winston Churchill's name to its credit, perhaps it is not
surprising that this outstanding conservation area looks
capable of weathering many a storm yet.

(ii) HARROW VILLAGE

Like its neighbouring area 'school' at the northern end of the
hill, Harrow-on-the-Hill 'village' ranks as an outstanding
conservation area. The southern end of the High Street
belongs to it and so do those old precipitous thoroughfares
called West Street and Crown Street, now the bane of every
motorist misguided enough to attempt them.

Picturesque almost by nature, the 'village' was saved from

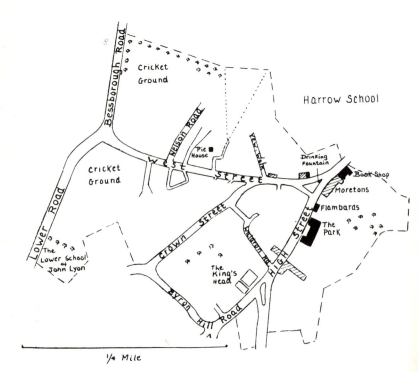

High Street

becoming part of the new town of Harrow for the simple reason that the railway station (Harrow and Wealdstone) on the London and Birmingham railway, started in 1837, was built a mile and a half away. Predictably the new town sprang up around the station and it never quite reached the windy heights of old Harrow.

For centuries Harrow village was the centre of a most thriving agricultural community. The Middlesex soil surrounding it was "excellent, fat and fertile and full of profit" – so good in fact that Harrow wheat, which grew abundantly on the hill slopes, yielded a particularly fine flour duly noted by Elizabeth I who used to take it in lieu of money as payment for her dues.

Against this favourable background the village grew, prospered and gradually changed and, although today its name is inevitably associated with that of the famous school, one can still feel the old identity asserting itself.

Standing on the east side of the High Street just beyond the point where the 'school' conservation area merges into that of the 'village', the house now occupied by the school bookshop is where the vestry meetings used to be held. It is also noted for its association with Sir Robert Peel who had rooms here during his three years at Harrow School.

The drinking foundation which stands perched in the corner above the steep descent into West Street just beyond the school stores was originally the old town well, sunk in 1816. Incidentally this well provides a clue to the geology of Harrow. When the shaft was sunk, 245 feet of clay had to be bored through before sand was reached and below that there was 200 feet of chalk.

Many of the large houses further along the High Street, including Moretons and Flambards, now belong to Harrow School but originally they were private dwellings. Flambards was built in the eighteenth century to replace an earlier manor-house on a nearby site and is named after the family who owned it. Some of the brasses in Harrow Church commemorate Sir Edward Flambard and his wife, *circa* 1390, and Sir John Flambard, *circa* 1442.

The house called 'The Park' which stands just beyond was built shortly before 1800 when Flambards began to be considered too small for the Barons Northwick. In those days it possessed extensive grounds with a serpentine lake, all said to have been laid out by Capability Brown. In the course of many travels, the second baron amassed a large collection of curios and here at The Park he entertained the celebrities of the day, including Nelson. The lion made of artificial stone that now sits facing the High Street was moved from its original place over the garden door in 1906. The whole estate of some forty-seven acres was sold in 1825 and in 1831 the house was acquired by Harrow School for boarding purposes.

The clue to the history of the 'King's Head' at the junction of the High Street and Byron Hill Road is provided by the swinging Henry VIII inn sign erected on the green in the middle of the road – a green which probably dates back to the earliest days of the village. The 'King's Head' is a rebuilt version, with additions, of an ancient hostelry burnt down in 1750. Some of its large solidly built cellars, reputedly dating back to 1535 when the inn was used by Henry VIII as a hunting box, belonged to the original building.

From all accounts the excellence of the hunting in the surrounding woodland was a major attraction even as far back as medieval times when the archbishops of Canterbury regarded the village as a regular stopping-off place on their journeys between London and Woodstock. It was here, in

1170, that Thomas à Becket came to meet the Abbot Simon of St Albans as part of a final but unsuccessful attempt to appease Henry II.

The boundary of the conservation area follows Byron Hill Road to its junction with Crown Street and then skirts around the cricket grounds belonging to Harrow School, taking in the old grammar school known as The Lower School of John Lyon at the south-western tip. The built-up triangle of land between Crown Street and West Street is where the annual fair and weekly markets used to be held.

An annual fair was granted to Harrow as early as 1262 by Henry III and by the fourteenth century it was a very flourishing concern indeed, lasting more than six hundred years, until its abolition in 1850. With most people engaged in farming, the weekly Monday market (also since abolished) became equally popular and provided the lord of the manor, to whom all sorts of tolls had to be paid, with a valuable source of income.

If one emerges from Crown Street into the middle of West Street's steep descent towards the cricket fields, it is easy to miss the two narrow lanes wedged in between terraced houses on the north side leading to the field known as High Capers. High Capers used to adjoin the old fair and was where the village amusements took place. It takes one past the strange little timber-roofed Harrow Pie House (enclosed within the precincts of an electric light works) up to the northern boundary of the conservation area.

Harrow Pie House is now regarded as an interesting specimen of fourteenth or fifteenth century domestic architecture and is believed to be none other than the old Pie Court which was always attached to a fair. The name (by which it has been known since time immemorial) is probably derived from 'pie poudre', meaning 'dusty feet' because disputants were not even given time to brush themselves down before being forced to appear before the judges. The Pie Court was a court of summary jurisdiction where offences were immediately dealt with and no case could be postponed.

Such links with the past are now recognised as an important part of old Harrow's heritage and maybe one day ways and means will be found of saving other small properties, many urgently in need of renovation, which lie scattered around this historic area.

9

Highgate and Highgate Village

Entrance to Columbarium, Highgate Cemetery

As one soon discovers, there is more to Highgate than steep hills, literary associations and handsome eighteenth-century houses. Gone is the old 'high gate' where tolls were levied on those using the highway between the capital and northern counties and submerged are the old roads beneath the new, yet the place still has the aura of an important gateway to London.

'High' gate refers of course to the position of the tollgate at the summit of the hill and not to its dimensions. The structure was in fact a long low arch which had to be removed in 1769 because it was not high enough to take heavily laden wagons. It used to extend across the road from the Gatehouse Tavern at the top of the High Street to the old burial ground which one can still see in front of Highgate School chapel.

In the fourteenth century Highgate was part of the Bishop of London's hunting park, with the famous road passing through it. This was the road where, according to tradition, Dick Whittington stopped in about the year 1390 on his way back to the country and decided to try his luck once again in the capital.

Luck may have played a part in Highgate's long established reputation for good health but the chief factor was its geographical position, more than four hundred feet above sea level. Because of this it acquired a leper hospital in 1450 and by the sixteenth century it was on the list of fashionable places among London's 'northern heights' where a nobleman might safely build his country mansion. Unlike several of its

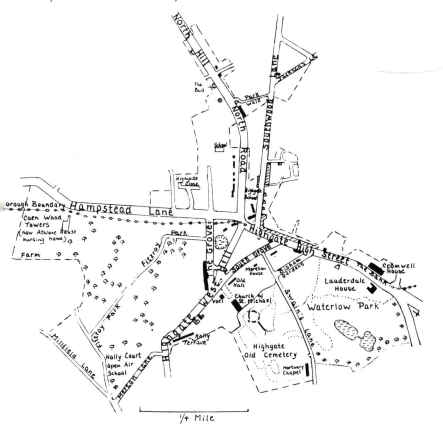

neighbours, it escaped the ravages of the plague of 1665 and further enhanced its reputation by establishing a children's hospital in its midst.

With these recognised advantages, the windy little village on the hill had turned itself, by the eighteenth century, into a small township centred around what is now Pond Square. Asphalted, crazy-paved and diminished though it now is, Pond Square was once a big pond in the middle of a large triangular village green – a green which covered the whole of the area between South Grove, West Hill and High Street and which became a recognised nucleus for the building aspirations of merchants and other successful people, some of whose fine houses still survive as listed properties.

Because the borough boundary line separating Haringey from Camden runs down the centre of Hampstead Lane and High Street, Highgate has two adjoining conservation areas instead of one. 'Highgate' lies north of the Hampstead Lane – High Street line within the Borough of Haringey while 'Highgate village' lies south of the line within the Borough of Camden. These arbitrary demarcations only appear of course on modern maps.

Since one might as well begin by getting used to Highgate's hills, a possible point of arrival is the underground station. Once across Archway Road, the north-eastern tip of the Highgate conservation area is only a few minutes' walk away, up Southwood Lane. Not all of Southwood Lane is included but if one turns off into leafy Park Walk leading into North Road, with its northerly extension North Hill, most of the route southward to the busy junction where the old 'high gate' once stood is conservation territory.

Transformed though this old street is into a busy modern highway, North Road still retains several fine eighteenth-century houses and forms a sort of central spine for the area designated by the Borough of Haringey.

The notice on the Wrestler's Tavern (modern version of an old inn dating back to 1547) at its corner with Park Walk recalls the ancient ceremony of 'Swearing on the Horns' formerly conducted at the Gatehouse Tavern. "Have you been sworn at Highgate?" was a question once familiar in all parts of the kingdom, the reason being that every traveller who passed through the village was expected to swear a somewhat whimsical oath on a bull's, stag's or other kind of horn and to acknowledge the inn keeper or person appointed to swear him in as his adopted father. The penalty for not conforming was a bottle of wine. Not surprisingly, by 1826 there were as many as nineteen licensed premises in Highgate, most of which displayed horns of one kind or another.

The attractions of Highgate clearly did not escape the notice of the literary community and, as the small plaque on No 92 North Road proclaims, Charles Dickens stayed here in 1832. Farther along on the opposite (west) side of this main road, A.E. Housman (1859-1936) wrote *A Shropshire Lad* while living at No 17. With its view across the road of Highgate School, this house and indeed the whole of the impressive terrace, Nos 13 to 19 North Road, of which it is part, dates back to the eighteenth century.

With its massive red brick chapel on the corner of the High Street behind the old burial ground, Highgate School was founded in 1565 by Sir Roger Cholmeley as a free grammar school "for the education and bringing up of youth in virtue and learning". The present Gothic-style building was erected in 1819 close to the old almshouses in Southwood Lane.

At this point the conservation area fans out at right angles, eastward along the High Street and westward along Hampstead Lane, with the Gatehouse Tavern (present

Cromwell House and Ireton House

building early 1930s) at the centre. The original inn, established before 1310, stood on the same site at the summit of the hill as did its Georgian successor, famed more for its fabulous 'ordinaries' dinners which cost one shilling a head than for the ghost which reputedly haunted the minstrel gallery. After partaking of "a bullock, roasted ribs of beef, a large goose or gander, two plum puddings, an apple pie and hot damson pie" maybe some of those who saw the ghost were not very reliable witnesses anyway.

Continuing to cope as best it can with the intrusions of excessive traffic, it is interesting to see that steep Highgate Hill, including the High Street at the top, still possesses several unconverted old houses including, on the north side, Northgate House and Ivy House built during the reign of William and Mary (1689-1702). Lower down on the stretch of hillside known as the Bank, the more impressive dome-capped Cromwell House, No 104 Highgate Hill, and adjoining Ireton House (No 106) date back to the seventeenth century.

The story that these two houses originally formed a single dwelling built by Oliver Cromwell as a residence for his son-in-law General Ireton is quite false. With its richly decorated staircase – there are marvellous little figures of seventeenth-century soldiers, including fifers and drummers, standing at the corners – and its fine ceilings, Cromwell House was built about 1640 by a merchant called Richard Sprignell or his son Robert. Ireton House was probably named after one of General Ireton's brothers who was a trustee of Richard Sprignell's will and it appears to have been built a little later.

In 1686 both houses were bought by the Da Costa family and remained in their hands until 1745. They were then occupied by various businessmen until Cromwell House became a private school in 1843. After a fire in 1865 had gutted the upper part of the building, Cromwell House was restored and taken over as a convalescent home by the Great Ormond Street Hospital for Sick Children. The hospital remained in occupation until 1924 when the house was acquired by the Mothercraft Training Centre and then by various missionary societies. Today Ireton House is still privately occupied but Cromwell House has become the headquarters of the Montfort Missionary Society who use it for training young men for the Catholic priesthood. On written request visitors are usually allowed to look round and given access to the rooftop platform, with its fine view of the surrounding countryside.

This is as far east as the Highgate conservation area goes. The south side of the High Street, with its own complement of old houses, notably Englefield House (No 23) and Nos 17, 19 and 21 built in 1733 as replacements for earlier dwellings on land that once belonged to Sir Roger Cholmeley, founder of Highgate School, is now within the Borough of Camden and forms the base line for the more extensive Highgate village conservation area.

Highgate village conservation area includes the whole of Waterlow Park, the famous old Highgate Cemetery and the exclusive wooded residential estate to the west known as Fitzroy Park.

The large two-storey house immediately opposite Cromwell House at the entrance to Waterlow Park is one of the most important and oldest buildings in this area. Standing behind wrought iron gates on the south side of the street, it was once the home of the Earls of Lauderdale but part of it, namely the long range facing south-east that looks over the gardens, is believed to date back even further, to the latter years of the sixteenth century. Some of the panels of the long ground floor of this range were found *in situ* and it is considered probable that the upper projecting storey was originally the 'long gallery' of an Elizabethan house.

The indications are that Lauderdale House was largely altered during the reign of Charles II and certainly the fine staircase with its elaborate and beautifully designed lantern is of this date. According to tradition, one of the early occupants was Nell Gwynne, the story being that on one occasion she held her baby son out of an upper window, threatening to drop him because Charles II would not grant him a title, whereupon the king hastily exclaimed, "Save the Earl of Burford"!

Lauderdale House was taken over by the London County Council in 1889 and put into good repair. Its two-columned porch of the Doric order leads to a hall which now serves as a shelter for those using the park, while the lower ground floor space on the south-east side has been turned into a refreshment room, leaving the upper floor to provide residential accommodation for council staff.

As for the park itself, this was a gift to the people of Highgate by a benefactor called Sir Sidney Hedley Waterlow, Lord Mayor of London in 1872-3, who wanted to give "a garden to the gardenless". With its delightful undulating walks and artificial lake down in the hollow, the park was formed from the grounds of Hertford House (now demolished) and its neighbour, Fairseat, together with the land belonging to Lauderdale House.

The steep narrow lane into which one emerges after leaving Waterlow Park on the west side close to the tennis courts and putting green is of course Swain's Lane, instantly recognisable by the high enclosing wall of Highgate Cemetery.

Alas, after years of neglect and recent attacks of vandalism, the old Victorian cemetery with its remarkable columbarium and other dramatic monuments to those famous artists, writers, scientists, inventors and well-to-do citizens of north London who paid so handsomely for the privilege of ending their days here instead of in the pestilential city burial grounds had to be temporarily closed to the public. The massive iron gateway is bolted and barred and it may be some time before Camden Council can complete its plans for the acquisition and re-instatement of this cold, lonely but fascinating place designed by Geary and first opened by the London Cemetery Company in 1838. In recent times a voluntary organisation called the 'Friends of Highgate Cemetery' was set up under the auspices of the Highgate Society with the aim of making it into a national monument. With the permission of the present owners (United Cemeteries Ltd), volunteers cleared the ground around the graves of the Dickens family, the nineteenth-century cricketer Lillywhite, the Rossetti family and the scientist Michael Faraday – graves which now all have GLC Grade 2 architectural listing. Some years ago the tomb of Karl Marx was moved to the newer cemetery down the hill on the east side of Swain's Lane, which puts it just outside the conservation area.

Swain's Lane itself is a very old thoroughfare. One of four parallel routes up the hill, it was mentioned as far back as 1492. Leading up to Pond Square and the surrounding groups of old houses and cottages, it brings one out into that part of South Grove once known as Angel Row – a row of buildings which stretched from the Angel Inn at the corner with the High Street to Russell House, No 9 South Grove.

Apart from its cemented front which belongs to the end of the eighteenth century, this low three-storeyed house was built about 1725-30, making it a little older than its fine brick-fronted neighbour Church House, No 10 South Grove, now occupied by the Highgate Society.

Moreton House, No 14 South Grove, began life about 1714 as one of a pair of houses but its companion was demolished years ago. Farther along still where South Grove meets West Hill, the larger and more conspicuous red-brick house known as the Old Hall dates mainly from a rebuilding of 1694, though it too appears to have been re-fronted at a later date. It was on this site and that of the adjoining sites now occupied by St Michael's Church and two seventeenth- to eighteenth-century houses (Voel and the demolished Southgate House) that the celebrated mansion of Sir William Cornwallis stood during the reigns of Elizabeth I and James I.

Set well back from the street behind the war memorial and forecourt, St Michael's Church was built in 1832 from the design of Lewis Vulliamy. Since it backs on to the wall of Highgate Cemetery near the columbarium, its tall tapering spire with finial and pinnacles is clearly visible in the south and east.

As the oval tablet above the attractive bar window indicates, some of the buildings of the nearby Flask Tavern date back to 1767. This is where the manor court sittings used to be held.

Instead of returning to the centre of Highgate via West Hill or the western stretch of South Grove (more often known these days simply as The Grove), one can, if in strong walking mood, wander off from the bottom of West Hill (just beyond the open-air school called Holly Court) into the Fitzroy Park estate with its new ranch-style and other modern houses set out attractively along the woody slopes of the hill. Although such habitations are in marked contrast with those of old Highgate, the whole of this estate and the lovely walk beyond as far as Caen Wood Towers has been included in the Highgate village conservation area.

Eventually the winding road brings one back to the well-trodden pavements of The Grove – very close in fact to where the Ladies' School was founded in 1667. This school, which occupied premises called Dorchester House, was not *for* ladies but was supported *by* ladies for the benefit of fatherless children and for "the diffusion of the principles of reformed religion" – principles for which Highgate has long been renowned.

All the houses, Nos 1 to 6, at the southern end of The Grove, including those which replaced Dorchester House, were built early in the eighteenth century or possibly earlier and, as the plaque on No 3 points out, the English poet and critic Samuel Taylor Coleridge lived here for nineteen years until his death in 1834. His modern successor in the literary field was J.B. Priestley who occupied the house for several years.

Nos 3 and 4 The Grove, built in 1700 with a communicating chimney, have the distinction of forming one of the earliest pairs of semi-detached houses in the country, while Nos 5 and 6 still retain their old fire insurance plates on their front walls – a reminder of the days when people had to depend upon the insurance companies to put out their fires and had to pay the premium for the privilege. No premium, no fire engine!

The enclosed triangular space between The Grove and West Hill is occupied by the Water Board's small reservoir but both streets take one back to the top of the High Street – to the spot where it would be so pleasant to stop, but for the risk to one's life, to pause and remember that here stood the tollgate that gave this historic area its name.

10

Holland Park

Remnant of Holland House

Beside the diverting blue building of the Commonwealth Institute opened in 1962 on the north side of Kensington High Street is the handsome but unobtrusive modern gateway opening into Holland Park – a park which now forms the core of one of bustling Kensington's most attractive conservation areas.

If it were not for the message of the notice board more people might hesitate to enter, for the long tree-lined avenue with the small cricket field on the left is still sometimes mistaken for a private drive leading to some secluded country mansion on the slope of the hill.

This of course is exactly what Holland House, surrounded by its great park, once was and what it might still be but for

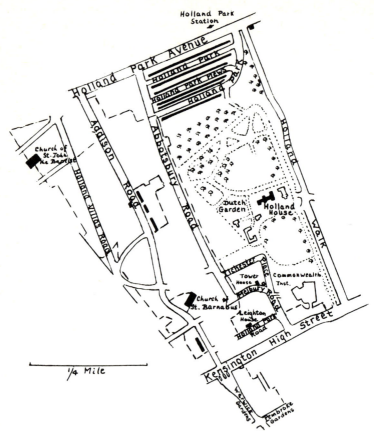

the tragic air-raid of September 1940. That night fire swept through the Jacobean mansion which for centuries had defied the pressures and encroachments of the encircling city, leaving only a token part of it to posterity. But fire could not destroy the fifty-five undeveloped acres and, remarkable as it may seem, these still exist today, including twenty-eight of beautiful woodland.

The eastern boundary of the conservation area is Holland Walk – the leafy footpath which follows a parallel route up the hill just outside the park. With its plentiful supply of seats and benches provided in recent years by the council, this footpath was given to the public in 1848 by the fourth Lord Holland by way of exchange after he had closed an ancient right of way that ran through the park in front of the southern terrace – a preliminary to his programme of 'improvements'.

As in the past, this or any route up through the park brings the old house quickly into view. It is true that Holland House is now but a shadow of its former self, with only the central portion (ground floor) complete with portico, arcades and restored east wing remaining, yet to many people it still possesses something of the quality of an old fairy-tale palace, just as it did hundreds of years ago.

Holland House began life as Cope Castle, built about 1607 for a recently knighted "gentleman of rare and excellent parts" called Walter Cope who had acquired all four of the Kensington manors. (The manors had been formed out of one original estate belonging to the Earls of Oxford.) The new owner sold off Notting Hill and part of the abbot's manor but kept most of the rest of the property, including this favoured plot on the southern side of the hill for himself. Here he built his mansion, entertained James I in 1612 and died two years later, heavily in debt.

After the re-marriage of Walter Cope's widow, the property passed to his daughter Isabel who had already married a wealthy and splendid courtier with the appropriate name of Henry Rich. In 1624 Henry Rich became the first Lord Holland and Cope Castle became known as Holland House. With its newly built symmetrical wings and arcades designed by the leading architect of the day, John Thorpe, its fame grew and so did the magnificence of its hospitality. The gate-piers of Portland stone which now dominate the approach to the reconstructed southern terrace are popularly attributed to Inigo Jones and were built by Nicholas Stone in 1629.

The row of brick arches which closes the vista of the Dutch Garden to the west of the house is another reminder of those distant days. They belonged to the old stables.

But not even the splendours of Holland House could save its master from tragedy. After wavering indecisively between royalist and parliamentary causes, the first Lord Holland headed an ill-considered rising in favour of Charles I and died on the scaffold in 1649 – an event followed by the confiscation of the house for use by the parliamentary leaders, including Fairfax. Reputedly this was their headquarters and tradition has it that Cromwell met his deaf General Ireton here in the grounds in order to conduct a shouting discussion on state affairs without being overheard. Hence the name given to

Ireton Lodge near the northern gate where the park 'governor' now lives.

Despite the continuing troubles of the Civil War, the mansion was eventually returned to Holland's widow who not only restored and extended it under the nose of the austere Commonwealth government but also established it as a theatre for the performance of stage plays. Thus, in 1964, when the London County Council inaugurated the staging of open-air performances of plays, opera and ballet every summer on the terrace, they were reviving an old tradition.

The next two seventeenth-century owners of Holland House both died young leaving child heirs and it is interesting to reflect that on the accession of William and Mary in 1688 the mansion narrowly escaped becoming a royal residence. The King went to inspect it but for some reason it was not to his taste and he bought the Earl of Nottingham's nearby property (now Kensington Palace) instead.

In addition to leaving a child heir, the second Lord Holland left an attractive widow, Charlotte, who was courted for a long time by Joseph Addison.

The influence on Holland House of Joseph Addison, whom Charlotte eventually married and who spent his last four years under its roof, was considerable. Whether or not his philosophical pronouncement that "everyone ought to reflect how much more unhappy he might be than he really is" had any bearing on his marriage is not known, but there is no doubt that he brought the house further fame by attracting other eminent philosophers and politicians. His name is commemorated in Addison Road – a separate part of the Holland Park conservation area farther west.

After Addison's step-son died in 1721 leaving no heir, Holland House had to be let. It passed through several hands and went into something of a decline before being leased in 1746, and later purchased, by Henry Fox.

Henry Fox was a patron of the arts and the father of the celebrated Charles James Fox who was brought up in the house. Among Henry Fox's protégés was Joshua Reynolds who painted the famous picture of his sister-in-law, Lady Sarah Lennox, the lady who refused to listen to the bashful addresses of George III when he passed by on horseback and saw her in a fancied habit making hay in a field close to the great road (now Kensington High Street). However, in spite of some amiable qualities, Henry Fox was not a popular lord of the manor. It is believed that he lined his nest with the interest on money he was supposed to be looking after as Paymaster General and that he also engaged in intimidation and bribery. His eldest son died only a few months after he did, leaving the baby grandson Henry to succeed.

This was the boy who was to become the third Lord Holland (1773-1840) whose seated bronze statue by G.F. Watts and Edgar Boehm now stands on the highest point of the estate at the centre of a number of radiating paths on the edge of the beautiful woodland, originally known as 'the Wildernesse', to the north of the house. And it is his couplet which adorns the little Dutch Garden alcove called Rogers' Seat, once the fireplace of the harness-room of the old stables. Lord Holland composed the couplet in 1812 as a tribute to the poet Samuel Rogers. It reads:

'Here Rogers sat, and here for ever dwell
With me those pleasures that he sings so well.'

Although the third Lord Holland's minority had led to some deterioration of the house, the situation was soon reversed after he returned in 1796 from his youthful travels accompanied by a vigorous and ambitious married lady who subsequently divorced her husband and married him.

Not even an initial show of antagonism could stop the new mistress of Holland House from turning it once again into a great centre of social activity. What with the continued influence of Charles James Fox and his fellow wits, Lady Holland's famous Sunday parties and Lord Holland's geniality, cheerfulness, intellectual interests and progressive attitudes, it was soon renowned throughout the capital as a popular venue for prominent Whig politicians and also, eventually, for the latest recruits to literature, including Dickens and Macaulay.

No doubt it was partly for the benefit of these distinguished guests that Lady Holland laid out the beautiful gardens with their box-bordered flowers to the west of the house. Dahlias were one of her specialities and it is believed that she was the first person to introduce them to England.

But this golden age could not last. In 1840 the third Lord Holland died suddenly and the era of development began which was to lay the foundations of most of the remainder of the Holland Park conservation area and the built-up area surrounding it. Up to this time there had been only a small amount of speculative building near the estate's western extremity (where the railway line is now) and even these changes had been deplored by their lord and ladyships. "An important but melancholy occupation" was how Lord Holland referred to the marking out of Addison Road when first leases were granted in 1824. (The leases were for sites on the east side of the road – sites recently redeveloped with second generation town houses.) The sentiment was echoed by Lady Holland who spoke of "our improvident reliance on them as sources of income".

The fourth Lord Holland was a delicate and reputedly a reserved, querulous but intelligent man who eventually, after his mother's death, came back from a life spent mainly abroad and mortgaged the house and grounds. Initially no doubt money was needed for the construction of roads and sewers but later on the cry was for 'improvements' to the house and the construction of elaborate garden buildings for entertainment purposes.

The conservatory – or orangery as it is often called – and the garden ballroom (now the Belvedere Restaurant), still standing conspicuously intact to the west of the house beyond the gardens, bear witness to this stage in the saga. Neither succumbed to the hazards of wartime which destroyed the great house itself and only in recent years, following a fire started by a disturbed waiter, was any substantial restoration needed.

The nearby park gateway was constructed by the London County Council to provide access to and from Abbotsbury Road – the long road running roughly north and south along the west side of the park. Abbotsbury Road was originally a track with fields on either side and was known as Green Lane. Now, together with the small group of residential roads south of the gateway as far as Holland Park Road, it marks the western boundary of the park section of the conservation area.

The names given to some of these residential roads, notably Ilchester Place (an attractive 1920s development of large houses), provide the clue to the next stage in Holland Park's history. From the beginning, the fourth Lord Holland had found both his mansion and the English climate intensely cold and he died a sick man in 1859, bequeathing everything to his wife Mary – debts, mortgages and all. In 1873 Lady Holland's financial affairs reached crisis point and, since this time there was not even a child to inherit, she decided to offer the whole estate to the fifth Earl of Ilchester in return for a handsome annuity. Lord Ilchester was a member of a wealthy branch of the Fox family and he accepted the offer.

The new owner took his responsibilities seriously in that he arranged for a thorough renovation of the house and saw to it that plans for the development of the area beyond its visual range forged ahead. Abbotsbury and Melbury Roads were both named after Ilchester estates in other parts of the country.

As the blue plaques indicate, Melbury Road became a residential area for prosperous artists. There was William Holman at No 18, Sir Luke Fildes at No 31, and the sculptor Sir Hamo Thorneycroft at Melbury Cottage (now demolished). But by that time the only really old house of note in the area other than Holland House itself had already

The Tower House

vanished. Known as Little Holland House, it had been replaced by smaller dwellings which in their turn were to give way to the block of flats called Woodsford.

Uniquely Victorian, the Tower House, No 9 Melbury Road, was begun in 1875 by the gifted and eccentric architect William Burges who lived here until his death in 1881. Inside its two-foot thick walls is a highly ornamental and sumptuous interior. After a period of decay when the house was unoccupied for four years, a preservation order was placed on it and in 1965 the house was restored and modernised. Today it is back in private ownership.

Close by in Holland Park Road, Leighton House now provides one of the country's most interesting exhibitions of High Victorian Art. One of the earliest examples of a purpose-built studio, it was built in 1866 by George Aitchison for Frederic Lord Leighton and offered to the nation by Leighton's sisters after his death in 1896.

On the northern side of the park, the conservation area extends as far as Holland Park Avenue – the old Roman road now transformed into part of a main route from London's western suburbs to Notting Hill and Bayswater. Development of the area between this busy highway and the park had also begun during the second half of the nineteenth century and by 1871 the residential road that follows an elliptical course and is confusingly known as Holland Park had already acquired thirty-six of its large white stuccoed houses. The remainder followed at intervals, right up to 1936.

However glamorous its present-day occupants, colourful cobbled Holland Park Mews which runs downhill between the two long sections of this road to meet the handsome gateway at its western end was, as one might guess, originally built for the coachmen and grooms of the late nineteenth century. From these picturesque dwellings with their external staircases, widely proportioned windows and crowning cornices topped by balustrades, the coachmen used to sally forth with their employers' carriages to await instructions at the appropriate front door.

The absence of a No 1 Holland Park is easily explained. After being badly damaged during the last war, the house was eventually demolished and not replaced. Instead the London County Council constructed the small gateway that leads into the park, together with the delightful little 'sun-trap' area just inside, complete with seats and flowers.

If one takes the path back through the woods, the reappearance of the mansion's fragmentary outline provides yet again a piquant reminder of the sad demise of the once great house. During the long widowhood of the Dowager Countess Ilchester, Holland House lay in tranquil retirement, with the sixth Lord Ilchester becoming more interested in the writing of its history than in its resuscitation as a cultural centre. Absorbing and creative as this occupation no doubt was, it did not relieve the new owner of the problems of maintenance, taxation and finally of the wartime catastrophe which turned most of the building into a ruin and which led, in 1945, to the London County Council being approached.

In 1952, after protracted negotiations, the LCC agreed to purchase the estate for around a quarter of a million pounds but the problem of what to do with the derelict mansion remained. By 1957, after many conflicts and differences of opinion, the decision had been made to save the east wing but to pull down most of the remainder. As the notices indicate, the restored east wing owes its present existence to the Youth Hostels Association, with help from the King George VI Memorial Fund. It was designed in 1955 by Sir Hugh Casson and, although some people think it less satisfactory than it might have been, it was generally accepted that some compromise was necessary. It now serves a valuable purpose and, with its faithfully restored tower, offers at least some hint of past glories.

Having made so unique a contribution to English social history, it is interesting to note that among the many present-day beneficiaries of this lovely town park are the pupils of Holland Park Comprehensive School whose extensive premises lie just outside the conservation area at the northern end of Holland Walk. There have been some cases of vandalism from this quarter but the gardeners declare that the culprits belong to a small minority. It would be sad indeed if it were otherwise.

11

Kew Green

Church of St Anne

There is an element of pleasurable surprise about Kew Green.
Overlooked by tower blocks from across the river and with
traffic roaring its way over Kew Bridge and along the main
road that divides the triangular green into two parts, this small
oasis of charm with its Georgian houses and stretch of
undeveloped river frontage seems like a world apart from the

twentieth-century noise and bustle pressing in around it.

Two hundred years ago the life of Kew Green was bound up with that of George III and his enormous family and one does not have to look far to see what this important epoch bequeathed to Kew. Several of the fine houses which still survive around Kew Green were once occupied by the royal dukes and by the various people who attended them. Even the sight of white flannelled cricketers on summer afternoons is a reminder that cricket has been played here since the eighteenth century.

Nor is it difficult to recognise other phases through which Kew has passed. The arrival of public holiday crowds at the entrance to Kew Gardens still reflects something of the old air of gaiety which descended on the riverside village when the public first began to be admitted to the Royal Gardens in 1840. In those early days part of the gardens were open on Thursdays and another part on Sundays, Sundays always being the popular day – a day when carriages covered the green and more than £300 was often taken in tolls at the bridge.

Gone are the strains of music from summer evening parties coming up the river to the ait (small island) opposite Kew Palace where the Prince of Wales lived, and gone are the high jinks that regularly took place on the green before the fair was abolished (because of rowdiness), yet all these things seem to

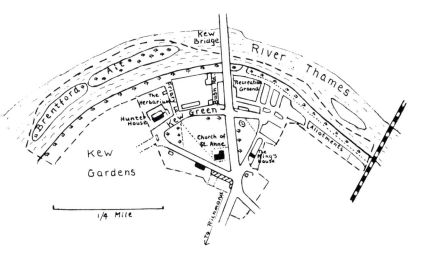

have left something of themselves behind. After the days of gaiety had vanished, Kew underwent a period of social decline but eventually re-emerged as the characterful suburb it is today with most of the original village nucleus and river bank now designated as a conservation area.

As one might expect, the church of St Anne, standing conspicuously close to the main road near the apex of the triangular green, provides many of the clues to Kew's history. The only pity is that, apart from special occasions including church services and afternoons during the summer from May onwards, this yellow and red brick eighteenth-century building, with its stone turret and cupola and later additions, now has to be kept locked for security reasons. However its graceful classical exterior with surrounding narrow strip of churchyard from which the tops of old tombs can still be seen peering over low walls is in itself sufficient evidence of its importance.

The story of the church began in the reign of Henry VIII, a time when Kew was still spelt Kayhough, meaning that it was simply a place with a quay ('kay') and that the land near the river was low ('hough'). Previous to that there are few documentary references to the hamlet and the only real clue to Kew's very early history comes from the remains found in the bed of the river near the bridge – finds which suggest that it was an old British settlement.

By 1522 however records had begun to appear. In that year a licence was granted by the Bishop of Winchester for the building of a chapel, indicating that by this time Kew was already becoming popular with several members of Henry VIII's court as a place of residence and was destined to grow into an elegant village.

Although all traces of the houses inhabited by the Tudor courtiers have disappeared, it is clear that the importance of the chapel in their midst had been established and courtiers of the Stuart period continued to use it. So important had it become that by 1710 the inhabitants of Kew came to the conclusion that it was too small and, with the support of the Vicar of Kingston, decided to petition Queen Anne, asking for a larger building. As lady of the manor, Queen Anne assented and presented the village with one hundred feet of land together with £100 towards the total cost of £500.

When completed and consecrated in 1714, the new church consisted of only a nave and chancel but it was enlarged in

1770 at the expense of George III and again in 1805 when the royal gallery was erected to accommodate his large family. In 1836 the church again acquired an addition – the west end with its pillaried portico, paid for with a legacy left for the purpose by William IV. Further extensions followed in 1884 and 1900, culminating in the new (1978) choir vestry.

In 1818 Kew Church was the scene of three royal weddings. The Dukes of Cambridge, Clarence and Kent – the Duke of Kent was the father of Queen Victoria – were all married here with some precipitancy after the death of the Prince of Wales' only child, Princess Charlotte, had high-lighted the need to strengthen the succession. (The profligate future George IV and his wife had formally separated soon after Princess Charlotte's birth so there was little prospect of a legitimate heir from that quarter.)

Regrettably the church records of these events are incomplete because in 1845 there was a curious robbery. An iron chest containing most of the registers dating back to 1717 disappeared and have never been recovered – a mystery which remains unexplained.

The narrow churchyard consists of the so-called 'old part' close to the church walls and an extra small piece of land granted by Queen Charlotte in 1818 known as the 'new part'. One of the overgrown tombs close to the south wall is that of Gainsborough. During the last few years of his life the great artist had a cottage in Kew but it seems that, locally at least, his talents were quickly forgotten. In 1816 a devotee came to Kew to do homage and asked to see his grave. The pew-openers did not know where it was but finally the visitor was shown it by the sexton's assistant. "Ah, friend," said the gentleman, "this is a hallowed spot – here lies one of Britain's favoured sons, whose genius has assisted in exalting her among the nations of the world." "Perhaps it was so," replied the man, "but we know nothing about the people buried, except to keep up their monuments, if the family pay; and perhaps, sir, you belong to this family; if so I'll tell you how much is due."

No such sad commentary appears to have been recorded concerning the grave of Johann Zoffany and his ponderous monument stands near by on the east side of the churchyard close to the main road. In the latter years of his life, after finally succeeding and becoming a rich man, the once struggling artist from Germany settled down not far away at

Strand-on-the-Green at the other side of the Thames.

The house with the large portico extending over the footway on the south side of the green is Cambridge Cottage, once the home of Adolphus Frederick, Duke of Cambridge, seventh son of George III. (George III had nine sons and six daughters.) After the Duke of Cambridge's death in 1850, his widow continued to occupy the house and her daughter Princess May of Cambridge was proposed to by the Duke of Teck in Kew Gardens. Like her parents before her, Princess May, who became mother of King George V's consort, chose to be married at Kew and her wedding in 1866 was attended by the widowed Queen Victoria, still in deep mourning. Cambridge Cottage, where she was brought up, is now used as offices by the Ministry of Agriculture.

Standing next door to Cambridge Cottage, 'The Gables' is one of several houses in Kew which has been re-modelled from earlier houses. It now belongs to the Royal Botanic Gardens – gardens originally started by Lord Capel and extended by various royal persons, including George III, and finally adopted as a national establishment six years before the large wrought iron gates which stand at the main entrance to the gardens were erected in 1846.

The rather plain looking mansion which extends some way along the north side of the green is the herbarium and library, founded in 1852 through the extensive herbaria of George Bentham and Sir William Hooker. The central part of the building was originally an old residence known as Hunter House but the four large wings were added later, in 1877, 1902, 1932 and 1969. The building now contains botanical collections thought to be the largest in the world.

The original Hunter House was named after one of its early owners, Robert Hunter, an eminent London merchant who died in 1812 and lies buried beneath the south aisle of the church. However Hunter was by no means the most famous occupant of this prominently sited house. That distinction undoubtedly goes to Ernest, Duke of Cumberland, otherwise known as Queen Victoria's 'wicked uncle'. After his mother's death in 1818 and with at least two sinister scandals behind him as well as a marriage to an 'unsuitable' woman, this most unpopular son of George III lived on in the house for many years – until finally departing to occupy the throne of Hanover. After his departure the house was known for a long time as Hanover House.

It is thought that the house, probably a country cottage, in which Sir Peter Lely lived stood somewhere along here on the north side of the green. Famous for his many portraits of the beauties of Charles II's reign, including one of Nell Gwynne, Lely was the first of the great artists to be attracted to Kew.

The iron railing that cuts across the west corner of the triangular green outside the herbarium indicates the site which George IV tactlessly took from the parishioners to incorporate into the Royal Gardens. It was not until his brother, William IV, succeeded to the throne that this plot was returned to the people.

Some of the houses with gardens backing on to the river which line the remaining north side of the green as far as the public house and bridge are Georgian. Apart from the church and a few fine villas in the vicinity, by the end of the nineteenth century this row of houses, including the Victorian infills still accounted for most of the village.

Even now, if one takes a winter walk down Ferry Lane, the fine solitary spectacle at the end presented by the long stretch of undeveloped river bank may come as a surprise. From here, the Kew Green conservation area, including the two islands known as the Brentford Ait, extends westward to just beyond the point where Kew Palace can be seen behind the walls of the Botanic Gardens, while in the eastward direction it extends beyond Kew Bridge to where the railway crosses the river. Since the northern boundary of the conservation area is drawn down the middle of the river, the southern half of Kew Bridge belongs to it.

With its three elliptical arches, this granite bridge was built between 1899 and 1903, the successor of two earlier structures. Originally there was only a primitive ferry between Kew and Brentford, but in 1758 the enterprising keeper Robert Turnstall decided that a bridge would be even more lucrative than the ferry so, with the help of the designer John Barnard, he set about the task of constructing one. Built partly of wood and partly of stone, the first bridge had seven spans. However it soon proved inadequate and between 1783 and 1789 Robert Turnstall's son decided to replace it by a stronger structure of brick and stone. With its eleven spans, this second bridge was designed by James Paine and Son and stood just east of the first. This was the bridge which eventually became known as old Kew Bridge – a great favourite with the artists who greatly deplored its eventual demolition.

If one follows the scenic route of the towing path eastwards under Kew Bridge, past the recreation ground, Victorian cottages, river tollhouse and allotment gardens to the railway bridge, one may well wonder about the island in mid-stream. This is Oliver's Island but it belongs to the conservation area of Strand-on-the-Green just across the river.

The network of attractive narrow streets and small cottages which bring one back via the pond to the stretch of green east of the main road is of course a Victorian development. No doubt it once helped to supply domestic labour for some of the larger nineteenth-century villas which were just beginning to appear side by side with the Georgian.

King's Cottage, No 20 The Green, near the post-office is one of Kew's oldest surviving houses. Formerly known as Church House, it was the house where the Earl of Bute lived. The Earl of Bute was preceptor to the future George IV and later became prime minister. He was responsible for a number of small dwellings known as 'baby houses' which were built at Kew and he was also a patron of William Chambers, the industrious architect employed by the royal family and renowned for the temples reminiscent of China and Italy with which he covered Kew Gardens. Another early occupant of King's Cottage was the Duke of Cumberland before he moved across the green to Hunter House. In more recent times it was the home of the retired Archbishop Lang.

The house with the green painted stucco is Haverfield House, so called because John Haverfield, superintendent of the Royal Gardens from 1766 to 1784, lived here. Haverfield's little daughter became the subject of one of Gainsborough's best known portraits, now preserved in the Wallace Collection – an interesting thought as one looks back across the road to the churchyard of St Anne where the great artist lies in a peaceful but neglected plot within yards of London's reverberating commuter traffic.

12

Kingston Old Town

Market Place

So vivid and colourful is Kingston's triangular market-place on a sunny day that one might almost mistake it for a stage set – a set where virtually anything could happen at any moment: the bells from the square tower of the medieval church could peal out a warning or a triumph, the gleaming gilded figure of Queen Anne could step majestically down from her balcony pedestal at the front of the Market House, or the whole area could suddenly erupt into some sort of operatic celebration.

Needless to say, a spot where such fancies are possible did not escape municipal notice and, with its narrow passageways leading down to the river on one side and to the old enclaves such as the Apple Market on the other, it now forms the focal point of the Kingston old town conservation area.

Centuries ago it is believed that Kingston old town stood at the centre of an extensive village green. With its pump and

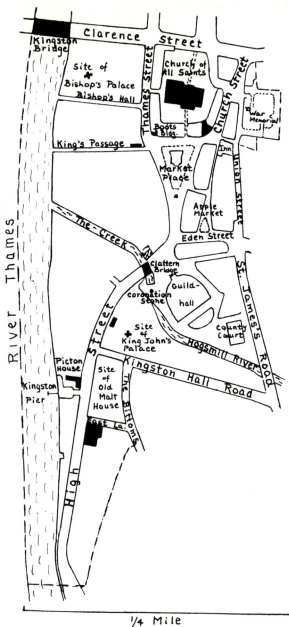

Clarence Street

Kingston Bridge

Thames Street

Church Street

Site of Bishop's Palace
Bishop's Hall

Church of All Saints

War Memorial

King's Passage

Boots Bldg.

Inn

Union Street

Market Place

Apple Market

River Thames

The Creek

Eden Street

St. James's Road

Clattern Bridge

Guild-hall

Coronation Stone

County Court

Site of King John's Palace

Hogsmill River

High Street

Picton House

Kingston Pier

Site of Old Malt House

The Bittoms

Kingston Hall Road

East Lane

¼ Mile

stocks near the main entrance to the church, the evidence is that the original green stretched all the way from the tiny tributary known as the Hogsmill River that flows into the Thames just south of the present-day Kingston Bridge to Water Lane beyond the Horse Fair. (The Horse Fair on the north side of Clarence Street is outside the conservation area. It changed its character after the old buildings surrounding it were pulled down about 1894 for street improvement.) But as time went on, the river frontage was built up and various other encroachments were allowed to develop, blocking out the river view and finally spelling the end of the actual green.

During the past fifty years the river bed and banks near Kingston Bridge have proved a happy hunting ground for those seeking information about the town's past. The finds indicate that even in prehistoric times there was a habitation here and that the Romans also made good use of the fordable crossing. However it was not until the arrival of the Saxons that fame descended upon the ancient hamlet. The Saxons called it Cyninges Tun, meaning the king's farm or estate, and crowned at least two of their kings here – Athelstan in 925 and Ethelred in 979.

Whether or not Athelstan and Ethelred, or any of the other five Saxon kings who are supposed to have been crowned at Kingston, ever sat on the so-called Coronation Stone that now stands mounted on its seven-sided pyramid, surrounded by pillars and protected by blue-painted railings near the Guildhall at the apex of the market-place remains, however, a matter for conjecture. There are many 'doubting Thomases' in Kingston today who cynically maintain that the massive monument is nothing more than a shapeless lump of old sandstone, but even if they are right, the Coronation Stone still seems to stand for something and its story is illuminating.

For a long time the stone stood near the chapel of St Mary – a small chapel which, until it was demolished in 1730, formed part of the church. Because of the demolition of the chapel the stone was moved to the front of the old red brick Town Hall where it came to be used as a mounting stone. But in 1839 this sheltering building also fell under the axe to make way for its successor (the building now used as the Market Hall) and the stone was simply dumped in the yard of the old Court House which stood on the site of the present Guildhall. Here it languished in obscurity until 1850 when a group of patriotic townsmen suddenly became convinced that it was in fact the

The Coronation Stone

long lost Coronation Stone and resolved to see it restored to a place of honour.

Restoration took place with due pomp and ceremony as the stone was re-erected on the platform above the Hogsmill River beside the old Clattern Bridge very close to where it now stands. With the names of seven Saxon kings cut carefully into the plinth, each with a silver coin of the right period (supplied by the British Museum) inserted above it, its days of indignity and obscurity were clearly over and, symbolically at least, it now remains as a permanent monument to Kingston's historic past.

Although no trace of a Saxon church has been found, it is considered virtually certain that one existed on the site where All Saints now stands. All Saints was founded in 1130 and was cruciform in shape until the nave aisles were added in 1490 and the chapels in 1460-80. After that the church began to look much as it does today – a large lofty rectangular building with some parts dating back to about 1300. Alas, a Norman west door discovered in the mid nineteenth century was merely photographed and then destroyed but since then much time, effort and money has been spent on preservation.

Perhaps the only criticism is that it was too heavily restored, the tower in particular. Originally the tower carried a lead covered spire but this was taken down in 1708 following fire and storm damage and the brick parapet was built.

Kingston market dates back to 1256. Granted as a crown concession for the sale of sheep and cattle as well as fruit and vegetables, it was held on Saturdays only until 1662 when a Wednesday market was also granted. Today, with the Market House at the centre, it is a daily retail market.

The Market House was not built as such but as a replacement Town Hall. Erected in 1840, it took the place of a red-brick structure from which nothing was saved except the gilded leaden figure of Queen Anne. The earlier Town Hall is believed to have been a refurbished and extended (1706) edition of the medieval Gild Hall – a timber and plaster affair on wooden pillars.

East of the church and market-place, the conservation area takes in the whole of Church Street and the War Memorial Garden, with St James' Road forming the rest of the eastern boundary southward as far as Kingston Hall Road. On its corner site, No 1 Church Street alias No 23 Market-Place has recently undergone major reconstruction; it is believed that the original building dated back as far as the fifteenth or seventeenth centuries. Until 1796 a smaller but similar building to the old Gild Hall also stood here at the entrance to Church Street.

It is fascinating to see how this eastern half of the old town, particularly where Crown Passage and Harrow Passage converge on the Apple Market, has retained its medieval air. The Crown Inn dates back only as far as the late seventeenth or eighteenth century but the small intimate scale and overall pattern of these narrow ancient alleyways with their overhanging storeys plainly belong to a much earlier age. One can well believe the story that a maidservant once escaped from fire by crossing from the projecting upper rooms on one side of Harrow Passage to the building on the opposite side.

By contrast, the semi-circular Guildhall and the new County Court behind it clearly bear witness to the age of redevelopment. Erected on the site of the old Assize Courts (1811) and of Clattern House (1777) which served during its latter days as a judge's lodging, a boys' school and a public library, this large municipal building was designed by Maurice Webb and opened in 1935.

Harrow Passage

Still the most important crossing over the narrow Hogsmill River, Clattern Bridge has very ancient foundations dating back to about 1180. Originally it was only eight feet wide and was called Bow or Stone Bridge. The present name seems to have been adopted on account of the clattering noise made by carts in the days of wooden wheels and cobbled surfaces. In

1850 the bridge was widened, strengthened, fitted with raised parapets and given its present ornamental railings to match those erected around the adjacent Coronation Stone.

South of the bridge, the High Street was once the town's old industrial quarter, originally called Westby Thames and lined with maltings on one side and wharves on the other. Throughout the many centuries when malt was big business here in Kingston, barges used to take the product downstream to London and return with other goods, including sea coal. But now that all the old malthouses and most of the other ancient buildings have disappeared, there are only three listed properties left in what could have been an area of outstanding historic interest.

There are indications that a palatial twelfth- or thirteenth-century building once stood in the area now bounded by the police station and Kingston Hall Road and that this was probably where King John, who granted the town its first recorded charter in 1200, stayed on several occasions. A stone column believed to have belonged to it was discovered last century in somebody's garden and now stands in the forecourt of the public library.

Although No 17 High Street (now occupied by London Steak House) has managed to survive since the eighteenth century, its former neighbour, a large handsome house dating back to Tudor times, was less fortunate. The house was known as King John's Palace because rumour had it that it once formed part of the ancient palace. However it was pulled down during the 1880s and replaced by the present shop property. That was the time when Kingston lost so many of its old buildings.

Perhaps Kingston's saddest loss of all was that of the old malt house – if only because it happened such a short time ago. The scene of the tragedy was the piece of land on the southern side of Kingston Hall Road (formerly Bittoms Lane), now fronted by hoardings and used as a car park. Here, until one November weekend in 1965, stood Kingston's last surviving malt house, built in 1517, side by side with eighteenth-century Grosvenor House (No 25 High Street). On the Sunday morning Kingston woke up to find that the old malt house and its neighbour, both supposedly protected by preservation orders, had been bulldozed to the ground, leaving nothing behind but the land on which they had stood and a sense of irreparable loss. How and why this was allowed to happen has never been adequately explained.

Still nursing its sense of loss, Kingston has since devised various plans for developing this ancient riverside street which stretches as far as South Lane and forms a potentially attractive part of the conservation area. The surviving jettied building, No 37 High Street (ground floor occupied by Moss Bros.) at the corner of East Lane, together with the adjoining property, Nos 39-41 High Street, dates back to about 1600 and is seen as providing at least one special architectural feature.

It is also hoped that in any development scheme, some use could be made of Picton House, No 52 High Street, on the opposite (west) side of the street. With a frontage on to the river, this neglected looking Georgian house was built in 1730-40 and was owned by a certain Cesar Picton who is believed to have come to England as a little black slave in the ownership of Sir John Philipps. Although Cesar Picton's master owned a house in Kingston, his ancestral home was Picton Castle in Pembrokeshire – which explains the name given to the boy.

In later years this old riverside house received various additions but the original structure can still be identified. Earlier this century it was used as a boathouse and family home for a certain Ben Pope before becoming a restaurant and tea gardens. Finally however when the up-river service by Salters Steamers came to an end, Picton House went into a decline. In 1970 the council, who now own the property, had plans for pulling it down and redeveloping the site as an Arts Centre but protests from local societies resulted in permission being refused by the Minister of the Environment. The necessary funds and some inspired solutions for its future are now awaited.

Back at Clattern Bridge on the west side of the street, one may wonder what happens to the dark water of the creek flowing beneath the parapet. Disappearing between warehouses, other riverside buildings and landing stages, this final stretch of the Hogsmill River has only about three hundred yards to go before it enters the Thames. Standing above it at the north side of the bridge, the two small houses whose ground floors are now occupied by shops are believed to have originated in the fifteenth century. Both however have been much altered and extended.

Although most of the space between the Thames and the market-place is now occupied by stores and warehouses, the old alleyway called King's Passage, with a recently restored house at its entrance, still manages to squeeze its way down to the water's edge. Diagonally opposite, parts of No 14 Market Place which forms an adjunct to the impressive Boots' Building date back to the fifteenth and eighteenth centuries. Although certainly no antique – it was built in 1929 – the Boots' Building itself is now affectionately regarded because it fits in so well with its surroundings and makes its own positive contribution to the colourful market scene.

The other narrow lane leading down to the river, with its entrance in Thames Street, is called Bishops Hall because until 1350 a house belonging to the Bishops of Winchester and used by them while travelling around the diocese stood here. After the bishops gave up this *pied-à-terre* in favour of the manor at Sheen, the site was gradually given over to commercial uses and for a long time a tannery stood on it. There are now plans for its redevelopment.

The boundaries of Kingston old town have been generously drawn so as to include part of Clarence Street and the eastern half of Kingston Bridge since it is thought that these contribute to its character.

Present-day Kingston Bridge, opened in 1828 by the Duchess of Clarence, wife of the future William IV, was built by Edward Lapidge who lived at nearby Hampton Wick. It replaced the so-called Great Bridge – a bridge which was in fact no more than a flimsy narrow plank-like structure on wooden piles that stood about fifty yards downstream. (The lead-up road still survives.) It was this wooden bridge that carried the army of Richard Duke of York into Surrey during the Wars of the Roses and again helped to turn Kingston into a place of strategic importance during the Civil War.

Perhaps it is because the medieval outlines of Kingston old town have remained virtually unchanged that such events still have a quality of reality about them as one wanders around the streets. Over four hundred years ago the Tudor historian John Leland described what is now the conservation area as "the beste towne in all Southerey" and it is interesting to reflect on whether one could find a better description even today.

13

Merton Park

Church of St Mary

If one enters the Merton Park conservation area from the main road (A 238) leading to Esher or Kingston, one may well pause to wonder why this small leafy and peaceful backwater clustered around a twelfth-century flint church was not swallowed up long ago by south London's suburban sprawl.

Situated only eight miles from Westminster Bridge, how did forty acres of land, bounded on the north by a busy main road, escape the destruction and careless development of the

nineteenth and twentieth centuries and emerge as a planned residential suburb of fine tree-lined avenues well before the era of the garden suburb?

At least part of the answer to this conundrum lies in the personal story of John Innes, a strong-minded Victorian landowner whose name was to achieve posthumous fame in the gardening world but who was in fact no gardener and indeed had no original intention of laying the foundations of a semi-rural estate or of preserving the character of an ancient village.

However one has to remember that many centuries before John Innes set foot in Lower Merton, as Merton Park was then called, the foundations of the village itself had already been laid. The name is of Saxon origin, derived from *Mere tun* meaning a farm on a pond or marsh. In about 1115, some two years before embarking on the famous but long since vanished priory on the River Wandle a mile away to the east, a Norman

knight called Gilbert built the church of St Mary where a
Saxon church had once stood, and so began most of Merton's
recorded history.

As the long straggling village grew in importance, so did the
main road passing through it. On the north side were the alien
fields of neighbouring Wimbledon and on the south side, as
time went on, was Merton's ribbon development with two
ancient lanes branching off in the direction of the church. It
was into one of these lanes that Nelson and the Hamiltons
used to turn on their journeys to church during the time that
they lived at Merton Place on the site of the old priory in the
years before Trafalgar.

Whether or not the village's association with England's
national hero played any part in John Innes' decision to make
Merton his home is not known but it is clear that when he
arrived in 1867 as the new owner of a fair-sized estate on the
west side of the village, it was in the role of a land developer
intent on building himself a home outside the London fog and
making a good return on his investment by persuading the
railway companies to bring their new main lines through his
land so that he could develop it in a manner likely to attract
large numbers of commuters. It was not until the railway
companies refused to co-operate, choosing nearby Wimbledon
instead and leaving Lower Merton to become a forgotten
backwater, that the landowner realised that these ambitions
could not be realised.

The manner in which John Innes eventually coped with his
frustrations by revising his plans, lavishing his affections on
his adopted home and by re-directing his enormous energies
towards the foundation of an estate far smaller and more rural
in character than any he had previously envisaged is a saga in
itself, but one does not have to go far to observe the results.

If one turns off the traffic-laden highway immediately after
the railway crossing (branch line from Wimbledon to
Croydon) into Dorset Road and then into Melrose Road
leading directly to the church, one sees an example of how,
even in old age, this paternalistic but enterprising Victorian
continued to try out new ideas. Conspicuous for their pointed
bays and other distinctive features, the row of semi-detached
cottage-style houses, Nos 4 to 20 even, that stand well back
behind long gardens are clearly not the work of the ordinary
speculative Edwardian builder. In fact they represent the
prize-winning entry in a national competition inaugurated by

John Innes shortly after the turn of the century for a design of house that would fit well into a semi-rural environment yet meet the needs of the emerging would-be owner-occupier of modest means who could afford £500 and no more.

The competition was won by a young architect called John Sydney Brocklesby who, unlike John Innes' long standing and more traditional resident architect, H.G. Quartermain, had travelled extensively abroad and was an exponent of the Art Nouveau style of architecture. The houses in Melrose Road were duly inspected by Queen Alexandra and orders began to flow. Brocklesby became an employee of the Merton Park Estates Company (established in 1873 by John Innes and his brother James) and later began to operate on his own account, leaving behind him numerous examples of his work throughout the area.

The old National School at the Church Lane end of Melrose Road belongs, as one can see, to an earlier period. It was built in 1870 with money left for the purpose by the 'hermit millionaire' Richard Thornton, a picturesque character who had made a fortune as leading underwriter of Lloyds and had moved, in old age, from Clapham to a nearby mansion (now demolished) called Cannon Hill House. Until replaced by the modern primary school close by, the National School served most of the children in the village, including those who lived in the cottages (south side built by Brocklesby, north side by Quartermain) of the adjacent cul-de-sac.

With Erridge Road serving as part of its southern boundary, the conservation area includes the whole of the churchyard as well as the vicarage field. Some of the old tombs around the front of the church date back almost three hundred years – notably the one enclosed by railings and built of solid stone, with its still decipherable inscription to William Rutlish. William Rutlish was court embroiderer to Charles II and he was important to Merton because he left £400 for "putting out poor children born in this parish as apprentices" – money which in the event was left to accumulate until 1894, when it was used to establish Rutlish School, now standing on some of the land left by John Innes.

The church founded by Gilbert changed remarkably little over the years and by 1400 it was established substantially as it is today. Rightly described as a church of solid simplicity, it still possesses much of its original framework, including the Norman door circa 1121 re-erected inside the north porch when the north aisle was added last century.

Among the church's treasures are the hatchments of Sir William Hamilton and of Nelson (presented by Emma after his death) and the bench on which the famous admiral used to sit in his box pew two rows back from the pulpit. In its present position at the front of the church, the bench is often used nowadays by waiting bridegrooms!

But perhaps the greatest treasure of all is the beautiful carved Norman archway that stands between the churchyard and the vicarage. This archway was discovered during the

Norman archway from Merton Priory

demolition of an old house on the priory site in 1914 and was re-erected here in 1935. It is believed to have belonged to Merton Priory's hospitium (guest house within the precincts) and, as far as is known, it is the only substantial surviving relic of that ancient monastery. Surprisingly, in 1977, despite vigorous protests from the local amenity society, a garage was allowed to make its appearance only a few yards away on the vicarage side.

Until moved to the plantation just outside the church gate, Nelson's worn mounting stone used to stand a few yards away beside the old red brick wall and entrance (now bricked up) of a seventeenth-century mansion called Church House. Church House was demolished many years ago and replaced by a modern house but the old wall survived and is now on the scheduled list. It encloses land at present used as a school playing field. Also listed are the late seventeenth- or early eighteenth-century wrought iron gates which belonged to the mansion and which now stand re-erected close by in this delightful old enclave.

The plain fronted yellow brick vicarage facing the wall where Church Path begins to narrow was built about 1800. In recent years various attempts have been made to develop the glebe field behind it, but for the present at least it remains the scene of grazing ponies and local summer fetes – a scene described by an environmental expert as "so unique for the suburbs that it should be retained at all cost".

Church Path itself, running westward as far as Watery Lane, is an old thoroughfare which, until shortly after the last war, contained a thatched dwelling (just beyond the vicarage) believed to date back to the time of Henry VIII. The terraced cottages, Nos 15 to 23 odd, between the Church Hall and the intersection with Mostyn Road were probably built between 1809 and 1823.

With its magnificent horse chestnut trees, the lower part of Mostyn Road is one of John Innes' earliest creations and it is interesting to see how it developed during his lifetime and since. First came the row of cottages, Nos 40 to 50 even, specially built by him for his estate workers, then the large Victorian houses designed by his architect H.G. Quartermain for well-to-do families, followed by Nos 17, 27, 29 and Flint Barn (now a convent) all built by Brocklesby, and finally the infills of the 1920s.

John Innes' Park on the west side of the road was originally the private grounds of the 'Manor House' which the landowner began building for himself immediately he arrived in Merton in 1867 and which he frequently added to once he had begun to assume the role and responsibilities of squire of the village. Unlike his final bequest (1904) to horticulture which was to arouse endless controversy, John Innes left the park specifically to the people of Merton, with instructions for the laying out of the bowling green, tennis courts and other recreational facilities. Although now owned and maintained by the local authority, it has changed very little in the past seventy years.

The rear of the house called Merton Cottage (now also council owned) next to the park's entrance lodge in Church Path dates back to 1734. It was purchased in 1940 by the Horticultural Institute and remained its property until it moved away from Merton in 1953.

John Innes' own large creeper-clad Manor House, now with its main entrance in Watery Lane, became part of Rutlish School in 1957 and is at present used as accommodation for the headmaster, staff and sixth form.

Watery Lane is marked on the earliest map of the district (1746) with a cluster of dwellings (demolished earlier this century and replaced by hospital and other buildings) around its northern end where it joins the main road. As its name implies, there used to be several streams in its vicinity. Nowadays, with attractive half-timbered Corner Cottage (architect unknown) on its west side and the group of Brocklesby houses (including Steep Roof where Dan Maskell the TV tennis commentator lives) on the other, it forms a natural western boundary for the conservation area.

If one turns back eastward via the short footpath into Sheridan Road, the vista that lies ahead covers virtually the whole breadth of the conservation area. With its long stretch of plane trees and holly hedges and its mixture of architectural styles, this beautiful avenue, intersected by Mostyn Road and Church Lane, was yet another of John Innes' early creations.

The three Flemish-style flint houses at the western end were all built by Brocklesby and so was the fine brick house with the central balcony known as Southover which stands in the middle of the triangular piece of land bounded by Sheridan, Mostyn and Kingston Roads at this north-western corner of the conservation area.

Early in the 1970s this important 'triangle' suddenly

became the target of a takeover bid (accompanied by threats of compulsory purchase) by the Greater London Council who wanted to demolish the six owner-occupied houses in order to redevelop with blocks of flats – a proposal fiercely resisted by the community at large. The final outcome of this traumatic episode in the history of the Merton Park conservation area is not yet fully resolved but the six houses still stand. Southover is being converted into four GLC flats and of the other five houses, two which still remain in private ownership now have the distinction of being marked on the local authority's conservation map as making "a special contribution to the amenity and character" of the area.

Busy Kingston Road has been less fortunate. Plagued for nearly forty years by road widening schemes and ultimately by plans for a major new highway, the buildings which line it succumbed to 'planner's blight'. Only recently (on economic grounds) was the latest scheme abandoned.

No 180 Kingston Road, on the eastern corner of Mostyn Road, dates back to 1797. It is owned by Merton Church and provides, as it has done for a hundred years or more, accommodation for "five poor widows of the parish". Farther along this ancient main road, near the end of Church Lane, attractive Dorset Hall which now provides flats for the elderly is also a scheduled property. It was built in 1770.

Because of its geographical vulnerability, the Merton Park conservation area has presented something of a challenge to its conservation-minded inhabitants and to the amenity group (The John Innes Society) which represents them. Yet, as most are aware, the determined spirit of the man who found personal fulfilment here still lingers.

Now in their maturity, the hundreds of trees and hollies which John Innes planted not only bear witness to a Victorian dream, they provide a small pocket of twentieth-century suburbia with a unique and priceless asset.

14

Northolt Village Green

Church of St Mary

The A 40 (Western Avenue) out of London is not renowned for its scenic interest, yet suddenly, over on one's right on the knoll of a grassy hill there comes into view a solitary old village church with whitewashed walls. With its red roof tiles capped by a bell turret and short spire, it stands supreme and remote as if still untouched by the distant roar of traffic and the enveloping pressures of built-up areas on every side.

Thirteenth-century Northolt Church is the historic nucleus of the Northolt village conservation area which lies some hundred yards north of the highway. No wonder the conservationist feels the beckoning hand and a flush of

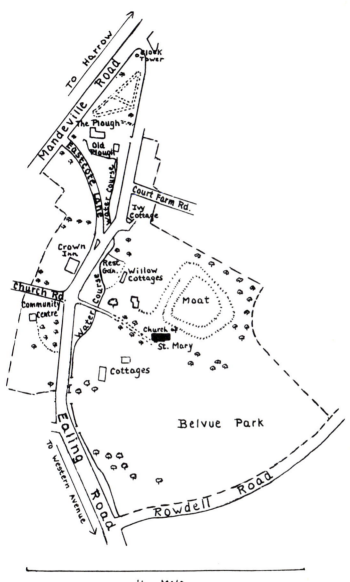

¼ Mile

pleasurable anticipation as the next roundabout heralds the turning (Ealing Road) that takes one into this small oasis of rural charm. In terms of environmental contrast alone, it would be difficult to over-estimate the value of such a bastion of resistance to the outside world.

The gently sloping land, now a public open space known as Belvue Park, on the east side of Ealing Road is part of the designated area. It is bounded on the south by Rowdell Road named after Henry Rowdell, once lord of the manor, whose well rubbed brass dated 1452 lies under the carpet beside the south wall inside the ancient church – a source of considerable interest, especially to American visitors.

Two centuries before the time of Henry Rowdell, the estate was owned by Peter de Botelier whose family held it for a century. Unlike their predecessors, including Geoffrey de Mandeville who is mentioned in the Domesday Book, this family actually lived in Northolt in the moated manor-house that stood adjacent to the church on a site dating back to Anglo-Saxon times.

Until the present century, Northolt was little more than an agricultural community and most of the land, with its scattered farmhouses, was laid down to grass for hay production for the London market, with only a little seasonal brickmaking as a diversion. The last lords of the manor were a family called Shadwell who appear to have pursued their traditional roles by keeping the village in a state approaching feudalism right up to the end of the Second World War – a factor which is now seen as contributing to its survival.

Whether one keeps to the main road, with its occasional groups of bungalows and cottages, or diverges on to the path beside the brook that runs alongside Belvue Park, the hillside church seen through the trees away to the east probably looks much as it has always done. Its importance both to the Northolt of the past and to the conservation area of today is easy to understand, particularly as the commanding quality of its presence becomes more marked from the openness of the central green.

After crossing the brook and climbing up through the somewhat wild looking churchyard with its old tombstones – among the more modern ones is that of the comedian Harry Tate who was buried on the east side under his real name – one might almost expect to find a view at the top of some coastal windswept moor. In point of fact the view to the south beyond Belvue Park and the Thames Valley is of the North Downs which can be seen quite well on a clear day.

Simple and virtually unrestored, the church of St Mary is the only listed building in the conservation area. It consists of a nave dating from between 1250 and 1290, a mid-sixteenth-century chancel and a porch and vestry of the present day. The west, north-west and south-west windows were all built about the middle of the thirteenth century, the north-east and south-east about fifty years later.

An interesting feature of the church is its off-centre appearance, typical of other small Middlesex churches. Here at Northolt this is due to the extension of the north wall of the nave at the time the chancel was built in 1540. Among the other more obvious additions is the shingled bell tower dating back to the late sixteenth century and the great brick buttresses which were built during the early eighteenth century to support the west wall. The font, which now stands in the nave near the south door – formerly it stood under the gallery built in 1722 – is late fourteenth-century work.

As for the north door, that was blocked out at some unknown date and is only visible from outside. It led directly to the manor-house within the moat and was obviously the door used by his lordship and his family.

The moat is now regarded as of considerable archaeological importance. It was constructed around 1350, though the site is very much older. So far only a few trenches have been dug but recent excavations on a small hillock of land have confirmed that an eighth-century Saxon village, with the usual complement of wooden buildings, once stood here. The archaeological finds already include a large Saxon sword and it is expected there will be many more discoveries.

As one follows the only footpath back down the hill, with grey-washed Deyntes Cottage on one side and the old National School on the other, it is pleasant to recognise some of the efforts that have been made in recent years to preserve and enhance this fine view of Northolt's central green with its superb oak in the foreground. The school, which was built in 1882, is now owned by Ealing Council and is used for Sunday school purposes and receptions, while the attractive rest garden just below the small adjacent parking space was laid out specially for the old and blind. The tiny row of single-storeyed cottages known as Willow Cottages, incorporated into the garden and now used for storage purposes, were only recently rescued from a state of oblivion and decay.

From any of these vantage points, the Crown Inn at the far side of the main road has long been an essential part of the scene. An inn has stood on this site since early in the eighteenth century. The present building acquired various additions during the Victorian and Edwardian eras and the best of the two architectural styles was retained in the recent portico extensions across the frontage. The bar on the northern side was formerly a stable.

As one walks up past the inn towards the two sections of the northern green, one may well wonder about the origin of the watercourse that runs close to the road and passes underneath it just short of Ivy Cottage before finally disappearing underground near the old 'Plough'. Surprisingly this agreeable little brook which is such a pleasant feature of the conservation area began life simply as a drainage ditch.

Still occupying its corner site and helping to divert the eye from the three shanty shops near by, tiny Ivy Cottage was built in 1820.

The post-war development to the east of Ealing Road lies outside the conservation area but the whole of the northern green, including both the old Plough Inn (now converted into flats) and the new Plough Inn are part of it. The new Plough, with its huge thatched roof and red brick walls, was built in 1940.

Conspicuous at the northernmost tip of the green, on a site formerly occupied by a rectangular fish pond, the clock tower was built in 1937 to commemorate the coronation of King George VI.

With a row of busy shops opposite and a major road immediately ahead, the clock marks the end of the Northolt village conservation area. It also highlights its vulnerability. Already beset by motorists taking short cuts between the two major roads and by attendant social problems, it is now acknowledged that some all embracing policy is needed to protect the rural informality of these pleasant acres whose trees and shrubs, village greens and ancient church were here long before the motorways and post-war developments were ever dreamed of.

15

Petersham

Church of St Peter

With its abundance of late seventeenth- and eighteenth-century houses it is not difficult to see why Petersham acquired its reputation as London's most elegant village-suburb and why nobody contradicted the Reverend R.S. Mills, one-time vicar of the old parish, when he declared that eighteenth-century England was practically ruled from Petersham.

Whether one walks around the narrow lanes gazing at the fine aristocratic mansions or visits the diminutive church and churchyard of St Peter looking at names on memorials and tombstones, the message is the same: Petersham was certainly not a village of nonentities.

Yet for all the power and wealth of its past inhabitants nobody, it seems, heeded the growing spectre of that arch

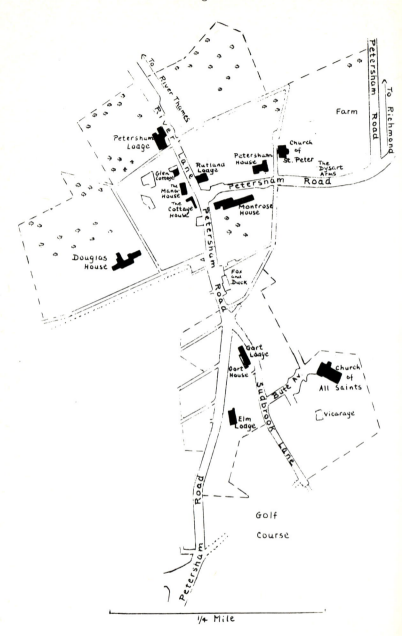

1/4 Mile

enemy – traffic. Part of the trouble springs from the fact that originally there was little to deter the owners of the great houses from building high walls around their grounds, thereby creating narrow lanes. At that time there was only a green track from Richmond Hill and even that came to an end at the stocks and pound where the 'Fox and Duck' now stands. The result was that even a hundred years ago, conditions were already difficult. As for today, when buses squeeze their way along the narrow Kingston-Richmond route and cars descend upon sharp dangerous bends at great speed, well, one can only marvel at the human survival rate.

Only a meadow and a small wood separate the northern boundary of the Petersham conservation area from the mighty Thames – the river which for centuries provided the village with easy access to London and no doubt accounts for its early existence.

Long before the Conqueror's men made their survey and called the village Patricesham, a Saxon church stood where St Peter's now stands in the narrow farm lane just off the main road. The Norman chancel incorporated into the present structure was built in 1266 but most of the building dates from 1505 when the church was rebuilt and from the seventeenth century onwards when the various 'enlargements', including the two transepts and galleries were added.

In spite of the so-called enlargements, Petersham Church is one of the smallest churches in Greater London. With its wooden steeple, its two-decker pulpit and old shoulder-high box pews still filling both the tiny transepts and galleries above, and with no clearly defined nave and no access to the south gallery and music gallery apart from the exterior door (1840) in the tower, it is also one of the quaintest.

Among the nationally famous who once attended Petersham Church were two prime ministers – Lord John Russell, who held a seat in the north gallery, and Gladstone. The historian Lord Macaulay was also among the long list of pew holders and so was the Earl of Cardigan who led the Charge of the Light Brigade at Balaclava. The famous eccentric Lady Mary Coke who invented the top hat and died in bed wearing one was yet another. As one might expect, the list of congregation members also included the titled owners of many of the great Petersham houses, including the beautiful Duchess of Queensbury of Douglas House whose self-willed arrogance once prompted her friend and neighbour Horace

Walpole of Strawberry Hill to remark: "... but thank God the Thames is between me and the Duchess of Queensbury"!

Such colourful figures all contributed to the life of Petersham – as no doubt did Elizabeth, Countess of Dysart (daughter of Sir Lionel Tollemache) when she married John Maitland, Earl of Lauderdale here in 1672. The bride is said to have been a great beauty in her time but much had happened since her first marriage: she had borne eleven children (six of whom had already died) and covetousness, ambition and pride are said to have "ravaged her comeliness and left their marks on her face". As for the bridegroom, he has been described as "a great gorilla of a man, with uncouth body and shambling gait, a massive head crowned with a disorderly tangle of red hair and when he spoke he slobbered". One can only speculate upon the scene at the altar after this ill assorted pair arrived with the Bishop of Worcester in their carriage for the purpose of performing the ceremony.

It is interesting to note that two hundred years later Petersham Church was the scene of a much more dignified society wedding, namely that of the parents of Queen Elizabeth, the Queen Mother. They were married here in 1881.

These days unfortunately the church has to be kept locked but the key can easily be obtained from a neighbouring house. Around midday when the sun pours in from the south window and the whole of the chancel becomes alight, one can hardly ignore the reclining life-size effigies in black alabaster of a certain George Cole of the Middle Temple and his wife and grandchild. This striking memorial was placed against the north wall in 1624, thereby blocking out an Early English window which can now only be seen from the churchyard. Also out of sight but by no means less present is the Earl of Dysart's vault beneath the altar wherein lies the remains of the remarkable Duchess of Lauderdale.

Among the lesser memorials that crowd the walls of this tiny church is one to Captain George Vancouver, discoverer of Vancouver Island. After his many adventures, the explorer finally settled down in Petersham in 1795, traditionally at Glen Cottage in River Lane, and died here in 1798 at the early age of forty. Like many illustrious people before and after him, he was buried in the churchyard. In recent years his grave has become the object of annual visits by a party of Canadian pilgrims who come to pay their respects.

The house with the Regency semi-circular domed portico upheld by Doric columns that stands on the main road only a short distance from the church is Petersham House, built about 1674 for Colonel Thomas Panton, Keeper of the New Park (now called Richmond Park). Its top storey was added when alterations were made in the late eighteenth or early nineteenth century.

Petersham House

The adjoining mansion with the fine door, gate and railings at the corner of River Lane known as Rutland Lodge was built for Sir William Bolton, a Lord Mayor of London, in about 1666 – a few years before its neighbour, Montrose House, made its appearance on the opposite side of the road.

Montrose House was built for the Recorder of the City of London about 1670 (Charles II's reign) but much of its elegant and detailed craftsmanship is of later date, belonging to the early eighteenth century when it was enlarged. It acquired its present name when it was leased by the Dowager Duchess of Montrose in 1838, twelve years before an unfortunate accident led to an action by the residents of neighbouring houses. In those days the boundary wall presented an even sharper corner than it does today and in 1850 a coach hit it, badly injuring the driver, passengers and horses. The resulting action was led by the Hon. Algernon Tollemache of Ham House who managed to extract a small piece of land from the owner in order to soften the angle. Today this handsome house, still standing on its precipitous corner, is owned by the dance band leader and pop star Tommy Steele.

Among the more interesting houses in River Lane leading down to the Thames, the manor-house prides itself on being a good example of Georgian architecture, while Glen Cottage rejoices in its reputation as the house where Captain Vancouver lived. The large white house near the river end was once the home of Lord Rochester and was later bought by the Duke of Clarence (the future William IV). The Duke owned four houses in the locality at different times and was a popular figure.

West of River Lane, the conservation area takes in the Douglas House estate where the Tollemache family have lived since they gave their famous Jacobean home, Ham House, to the National Trust in 1948. Ham House itself lies outside the eastern boundary of the Petersham conservation area but part of the old carriageway (now for pedestrians only) leading from the main road is included. Conspicuous because of its picturesque gateway, the carriageway also provides private access to Douglas House.

If one feels like deploring the passing of an age here in Petersham, it may be worth reflecting that such a sentiment is not new. The seventeenth-century antiquary John Aubrey, who was recommended by the diarist John Evelyn to visit the place, wrote deploring the fact that certain privileges had been lost. He described the village as "formerly a priviledg'd Place, as is plain from Records in the Tower of London, so that none could be arrested here, or one arrested in any other Place could not be brought through this Place, but through the long and scandalous Neglect this valuable Privilege is lost".

During the air raids of the Second World War many original documents relating to properties in Petersham and neighbouring Ham were lost but most of the houses within the conservation area speak for themselves. Several of those that lie in the triangle between the main Petersham Road and the northern end of Sudbrook Lane are on the scheduled list. Gort House was built in 1674 and much enlarged in 1800. Elm Lodge was built at the end of the eighteenth or early nineteenth century and was rented by Dickens during the summer of 1839 whilst he wrote the major part of *Nicholas Nickleby*. At that time literary giants such as Dickens and Thackeray were well aware of the attractions of Petersham and spent a lot of time in the village absorbing local colour for their books.

The conservation area does not extend far enough south along the main road to include the "genuine Tudor house" which puzzles so many people. This house has never appeared in the records for the simple reason that it was transported here several years ago, brick by brick, from its original home in Kent.

The wooded area to the east of Sudbrook Lane, including the red-brick church of All Saints, is however conservation territory. With its Italianate campanile and dark red brick interior, this church was built early in the present century by a wealthy woman resident.

Even now, as modest modern developments creep in, blocking out old vistas, it is interesting to see that wealth is still an important factor in this old Surrey village and must remain so if the great houses are to be properly maintained. The local borough council is always anxious to find owners or occupiers willing to co-operate in supporting the conservation principle. If they succeed, as so far they have done, Petersham's traditional "air of splendid superiority" will no doubt continue to exist for all who wish to breathe it.

16

Pinner High Street

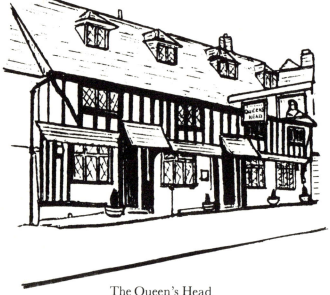

The Queen's Head

As one turns off the busy A 404 highway, it is suddenly there –
a real village street on gently rising ground with an old inn,
gabled shops, houses of Georgian vintage or earlier and an
ancient church at the head. What more could the connoisseur
of conservation areas ask of any street?

Pinner High Street owes its unusual width and character to
the fact that for centuries it served as a market-place and as a
site for the annual fair granted in 1336 by Edward III and it is
still going strong. The church was built in 1321 and ever since
1637, when its massive fifteenth-century clock tower acquired
its original cross, it has been a well-known landmark. At first it
led people through the surrounding forests, just as now it
helps guide them through the labyrinth of surrounding
suburbia. In 1958 the original tower cross had to be taken

down but it was replaced by the present laminated oak one of similar height.

How Pinner came by its name is not known for certain but, since 'ora' means river bank, it is generally assumed that this was once 'Pinna's settlement on the banks of the river'. Documents of 1232 concerning a certain Alfwin, who succeeded to his father's house and estate of two hundred acres of land, refer to it as 'Pinnora'. The valley route of the River Pinn was probably once of considerable importance to wandering tribes.

Together with the railway line, this little river helps to enclose the western part of the conservation area before the boundary swings eastward around Church Farm and Paine's Close at the northern end of the High Street. Many of the shop properties at this western (Marsh Road) end of the street, including the old white-washed cottage now known as The Victory public house, are on the scheduled list.

'The Victory', whose inn sign is inscribed with the year 1580 beneath a picture of a sailing ship, became a public house in 1951, taking its name from demolished premises (originally known as 'The Ship') in nearby Marsh Road. Before then the building was occupied by small shops, including a barber's. Although the additions at the rear of the building are modern, the corner post that stands outside still bears witness to the great age of a façade which only escaped demolition as a result of public outcry. The post was formed from an upturned tree trunk.

The two very old shop premises facing 'The Victory' on the opposite (north) side of the street are also survivors from the past. In their case, the chief enemy was a disastrous fire in 1891 which destroyed several of the adjacent properties. No 7 High Street (now a butcher's shop) is dated 1721 and No 11 (now the Old Oak Tea Rooms), which was weather-boarded until 1912, is a much restored wood-framed house dating back to the sixteenth century where a succession of parish clerks lived, including a Mr Bedford who is said to have slept on the premises every night of his life for eighty-five years.

No 25 High Street (now the village craft shop) is another of Pinner's fine old domestic properties built in the eighteenth-century, and so is the pleasant red brick and tile house No 27 next door which was occupied for two hundred years by a family of wheelwrights called Beaumont. The small plate attached to the wall beneath the gutter on the left, showing a

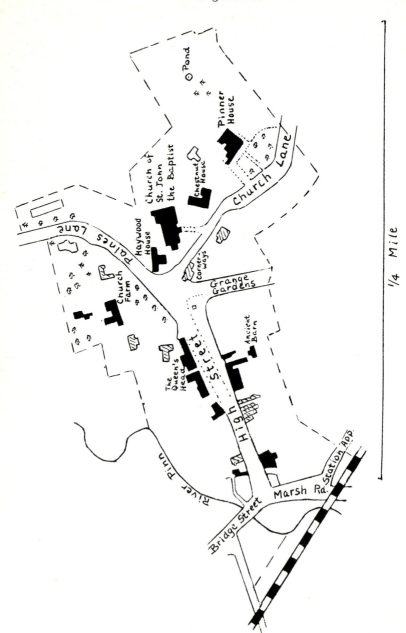

sun against a blue background, is the fire insurance plate supplied about two hundred years ago by the Sun Assurance Company.

A similar plate above the door of the red-brick house No 32 opposite shows that the 'Sun' had at least one other Pinner client on its books in the days (up to the 1830s) when premiums had to be paid to secure the services of a fire engine. Built about 1750, this elegant classical-styled house on the south side of the High Street was once a school, then a shop, and is now privately occupied. Like its timber-framed neighbours, Nos 26, 34 and 36, it is among Pinner High Street's many listed buildings.

The somewhat inaccessible ancient barn at the back of Nos 36 and 38 is also on the scheduled list. There used to be several such barns in the vicinity – an indication of the importance of Pinner market.

Returning to the north side of the widening High Street, it is interesting to reflect that one of the older properties, No 29 (now an antique shop) may have been Nell Gwynne's final home. If the tradition is true, the lady was no doubt well served by the inn next door.

The origins of 'The Queen's Head' date back to the late sixteenth century or beyond. It is thought that the original 'Queen' may have been Queen Philippa, wife of Edward III, though it was Queen Anne who changed horses here in 1705 on her way to Windsor and has been portrayed on the inn sign ever since. Until the 1830s, the inn had a plain plastered front and, until it was altered in the 1930s and turned into the carefully restored half timbered building with projecting upper storey that it is today, there were railings at the front and a porch with seats.

During the 1830s the seats were probably very useful for waiting travellers because this was the starting point for the Pinner coach which left every morning at 7.30 a.m. for London, arriving back at about 6 p.m. Later on, from 1886 to 1914, a horse bus operated six times a day between the inn and the station at Hatch End and in the hunting season the meets also used to start here.

No one so far appears to have substantiated the claim of The Old Bakery just beyond the inn that it was established in 1480 but here in Pinner High Street one may well feel that nothing is beyond the bounds of possibility. The nearby shop, originally known as Rossingtons (now Clegg the Tailor), is where Eleanor Ward, unmarried granddaughter of Lord Nelson, died after being knocked down by a runaway horse in 1872. She and her mother, Horatia Nelson Ward, lived for many years in the Pinner area.

As the tablet on one of the tree trunks records, the chestnut bordered triangular plot of land in front of Church Farm was given to the village in 1924 by John Edward Clark in order that it might be preserved in perpetuity as an open space for the benefit of the inhabitants of Pinner. It was once a village green, the only one left in Pinner after the Enclosure Act of 1803.

Despite its shingled walls and somewhat modern appearance, the long low building with the tiled roof known as Church Farm is a mixture of seventeenth- and eighteenth-century architecture. The east end, which probably replaced an earlier building, is the oldest part, the north and west wings having been added about a century later. This house is still noted for its beautiful old oak floor and for its oak and chestnut beams. However there appears to be no confirmation of the tradition that a bricked up passage in the cellar wall leads to the church. Such a passage, if it existed, would have to pass under the road and under the renovated building now called Haywood House.

It is thought that Haywood House may have been one of several houses seized by the church during the reign of Edward VI. The gabled part was added about 1878 by a Judge Barber who turned it into a temperance club called Ye Cocoa Tree Coffee Tavern which, as time went on, attracted people from all over London and even farther afield. By 1931 however it had become the premises of the Conservative Club and remained so until 1965. It is now used as offices.

One may well wonder about the small timbered building called 'Cornerways' which protrudes so prominently on to the High Street from its corner between Church Lane and Grange Gardens. This Tudor-style building, now a cafe, is thought to have been the home of a well-known local family called Bellamy, but it was taken over by the churchwardens in 1740. For three generations it served as a butcher's shop and the new windows and decorative timbering were not added until the 1920s. No doubt this innovation set the trend for the mock-Tudor (1931) Grange Court flats on the opposite corner of the High Street with Grange Gardens.

The church itself, still firmly and authoritatively entrenched

Cornerways and church of St John

at the head of the High Street, stands on the site of an old earthworks where a pagan shrine probably once stood before being superseded by an early Christian chapel. Although the clock tower dates back to the fifteenth century, the clock face is seventeenth century and the actual clock, which replaced an earlier one, is dated 1845. The church's fifteenth-century south porch was drastically restored in 1880 but in spite of these and other changes, including a 1958 facelift to the interior, Pinner Church continues to be renowned for its dignified and undiminished simplicity.

The somewhat alarming looking twenty-foot high monument in the churchyard near the south porch is known as the Loudon Monument. It has been described as the "coffin above ground" because the inscription tablets protruding from it remind some people of a coffin. It was erected by John Claudius Loudon, a celebrated horticulturist, in memory of his parents. Other graves include those of three centenarians, one of whom reached the ripe old age of 118.

Church Cottage on the south side of Church Lane contains part of an old building, possibly seventeenth century, while attractive gabled and plastered Chestnut Cottage on the north side is believed to incorporate parts which date back even further, to the sixteenth century.

The conservation area extends far enough eastward along Church Lane to include the fine three-storeyed red-brick house with five bays that stands well back from the road on the brow of the hill. This is Pinner House, said to have been built over a timber frame and dated 1721, though the deeds are 1838. The first curate of Pinner lived here at a time when there was no vicarage and when the grounds extended northward as far as Paine's Lane. From 1948 to 1972 the house was used as an old people's home but was then threatened with demolition. Only recently were plans passed allowing for some development of the land in order to pay for the re-establishment of the house as a home for the elderly. Understandably however the erection of modern bungalows aroused opposition and many conservationists were particularly incensed by the felling, despite preservation orders, of the fine old chestnut trees leading up to the pond.

The High Street Improvement Scheme started in 1966 and supported by the Pinner Association was a very successful but less controversial project. Indeed, as one walks back down this ancient street, one can only marvel at the degree of harmony and concentrated visual pleasure still afforded by this splendid little conservation area beside the River Pinn.

17

Richmond

Old Palace and Gate House

(i) THE GREEN

With fragments of the Old Palace and an abundance of Georgian and early Victorian houses clustered around one of the finest historic greens in England, it is hardly surprising that the Richmond Green conservation area has been classified as outstanding.

The name given to these few special acres, and indeed to the hundreds that lie beyond, is of course bound up with the great palace whose gilded splendour once graced the panoramic site between river and green and brought fame and riches to a whole region.

Rebuilt by Henry VII, Richmond Palace arose out of the fire-gutted remains of Sheen Palace, first occupied by Henry I and subsequently enlarged by Henry V. As the new version neared completion at the end of the fifteenth century, Henry

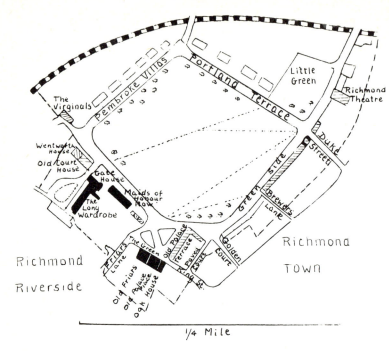

1/4 Mile

VII remembered his early life as Earl of Richmond in Yorkshire and decided that this was the right name for his royal creation. Possibly he foresaw that the name he chose would echo down the centuries but could he also have guessed that one day, when the remains of his palace were no more than a place of summer pilgrimage for countless London souls, people would declare that they could still detect something of the old dream-like quality?

Perhaps part of the quality of this historic and aesthetic centre of Richmond is the suddenness with which it appears – particularly if one emerges out of one of the ancient alleyways (now the delightful venue of antique, curio and flower shops) leading off the main shopping street.

Here, as the vista opens up before one's eyes, is one of the largest village greens left in England, flanked on the north-west and north-east by the Victorian and modern terraces and on the south-west by the famous Maids of Honour Row, with the original Tudor brick archway leading into Old Palace Yard just beyond. And as if this did not provide interest and variety enough, round to one's right near the eastern corner of the green, past some of the oldest houses in Richmond, is the contrasting Baroque-styled building, with its terracotta façade and green onion caps, of Richmond Theatre.

In medieval times Richmond Green was a jousting place and even by the middle of the sixteenth century when it still converged into waste or common land in the direction of Kew where sheep were allowed to graze, archers continued to exercise their traditional rights to practise on it. However by 1649 when a survey was taken of these "twenty acres of level turf" – today there are only eleven and a half acres – it had been planted out with more than a hundred elms and was described as "a special ornament to the town". With these and other embellishments and with few houses yet to be seen, the green soon turned itself into a fashionable promenade for London's quality and wits, though the age of development was not far away.

Fortunately for Richmond Green, the main development came at a time when domestic architecture was at its best and most of the fine houses that were built, many of which still survive today as homes or offices, fitted in well with their surroundings and with houses already there.

One of the houses already there was No 1 Green Side on the Richmond Town side of the green. With its gables and dormer windows, this is one of the oldest houses in Richmond, the tradition being that it belonged to Shakespeare's friend Simon Bardolph and that Shakespeare often stayed here when performing at the palace. The façade of its Gothic and embattled neighbour No 3 Green Side also conceals a very old house with Elizabethan and Jacobean features and there is little doubt about the originality of the carved wood cherubs' heads and foliage which adorn the fine door-cases of some of its other neighbours, Nos 11 and 12 in particular.

Much of the late seventeenth- and early eighteenth-century development took place on the adjacent south-west side of the green not far from Old Palace and includes the cluster of houses set well back behind the triangular grass verges before one reaches Maids of Honour Row.

Belonging to this cluster, sedate and graceful Old Palace Terrace at right angles to the green was built during the reign of Queen Anne (1702-14) and so too, probably, was Oak House, plain but conspicuous by its massively supported porch facing the green. Old Palace Place with the striking facade and fine front door that stands next to Oak House was probably earlier.

Completing this group east of Friars Lane, the house with the mellow deep red bricks and small sunken garden in front known as 'Old Friars' was built, like several other later buildings in the vicinity, on the foundations of the Convent of the Observant Friars – a monastery established by Henry VII adjacent to his palace. Old Friars made its appearance in the late seventeenth century, probably in 1687, though the long low building with Venetian windows that joins the main part to a smaller house or annexe was not added until about fifty years later. It is thought that the addition may have been "the Great Room on the Green" – a concert hall mentioned in newspaper advertisements in 1720.

The two houses called Tudor Lodge and Tudor Place which stand just beyond this interesting little enclave on the other side of Friars Lane, looking directly on to the green, once formed a single dwelling. They are believed to date back to the seventeenth century – somewhat earlier than the famous neighbouring terrace of four houses built in 1723 by command of George I to accommodate the Maids of Honour to Caroline, Princess of Wales.

At the time when Maids of Honour Row was built, Princess Caroline was living at Kew and apparently there was nowhere else in the town considered suitable for these ladies of the Court, all of whom received £200 a year plus board and lodging and enjoyed the dignity of being addressed as Mistress despite the fact that they were unmarried! The tradition that the residents of this fine terrace were very fond of sweet cheese cakes accounts for the continuing popularity of the 'Maids of Honour tartlets' still baked in Richmond today according to an old recipe.

If one decides to by-pass Old Palace Yard for the moment, it is interesting to know that the remaining two houses on this side of the green (immediately beyond the famous Tudor archway) began life in the early eighteenth century with flat fronts similar to those of Maids of Honour Row. Old Court House acquired its bow windows near the end of the century and Wentworth House underwent its Victorian transformation much later.

The Virginals, formerly known as Cedar Grove, which stands across the corner of Old Palace Lane (an ancient way leading down to the river) was rebuilt in 1813. The original

Maids of Honour Row

house, occupied by a French *émigré*, was built on the site of the king's bakehouse whose cellars led to the palace. Some of these cellars, though now blocked off, are said still to exist.

On the rather shabby north-west side of the green, Pembroke Villas are so named because they replaced the early eighteenth-century Pembroke House, home of the eccentric bachelor peer and recluse, Lord Fitzwilliam. Lord Fitzwilliam initiated the Handel festivals and when he died in 1816 he left his famous library and treasures to the University of Cambridge. In 1850 the house was bought by a builder who pulled it down and sold most of the ground to the railway company for the construction of the section of line between Richmond and Twickenham which now marks the northern boundary of the conservation area.

A hundred years later it was the turn of the north-west side of the green to bow to the demands of 'progress' and, to the expected accompaniment of objections, the row of functional looking dark grey modern houses with staggered elevations appeared on the scene side by side with what was left of Portland Terrace.

The piece of land called Little Green at the end of Portland Terrace was originally a piece of waste land granted by Charles II for use as a bowling green and was later used by the poor of Richmond. However in 1765 it became part of George III's royal garden and, like the rest of the green, has belonged to the Crown ever since, though the public has continued to have the right to use it.

Perhaps it is because the public have had the right to use Richmond Green for so long that it has always aroused such strong emotions. This was certainly the case when Richmond Theatre of the green onion caps was built in 1899. Standing on the extension of Green Side and overlooking Little Green, the building was seen, and still is by many people, as breaking the pattern of the green. Over the years it has been showered with uncomplimentary epithets such as 'blowsy', though its admirers continue to regard it as "a refreshing influence". Whichever school of thought one subscribes to, the theatre is now a familiar and accepted landmark and its value as a social asset to the old town is well recognised.

The long diagonal path across the middle of the green takes one back to the focal point of this historic area. Recently restored by the Crown Comissioners, Henry VII's archway is now nearly five centuries old, yet it still reveals the shadowy outline of the king's arms in sculptured stone.

The archway was the original entrance to the Middle Court, familiar to kings and queens and to other prominent figures of the day, including Cardinal Wolsey. After Wolsey had hurriedly relinquished his newly built home, Hampton Court, in favour of his envious lord and master Henry VIII, he was invited to use Richmond Palace.

Although the archway now leads into a small quiet square instead of into a Tudor courtyard, it is hardly surprising that legends continue to thrive here. According to one such legend, the narrow passage or apartment above the archway was where Queen Elizabeth died in 1603.

Until 1939, when it was converted into a separate house, the adjoining Gate House formed part of the large building known as Old Palace. There were then thirty odd rooms joined by tortuous passages. Restoration of the constelled parapets above the large semi-octagonal bays and deeply recessed mullioned windows has been an important part of the work recently carried out but quite a lot of the brickwork of the façade, with its faint black diamond-shaped cheeks, is original.

The impressive mellow yellow brick building with the steep tiled roof, ball ornaments and Tudor chimneys which stands just inside Old Palace Yard on the left is still known as the Long Wardrobe but it is now leased by the Crown as three private residences. In Tudor times the wardrobe was used for storing articles such as furniture and hangings and this one at Richmond Palace has survived because it was restored or rebuilt during the late seventeenth or early eighteenth century.

Originally the Privy Garden occupied the land immediately behind the wardrobe where the small group of houses, similarly leased by the Crown, now stand. However the house facing the archway, known as Trumpeter's House, belongs to the adjacent conservation area of Richmond Riverside, so here Richmond Green ends – at a spot still full of the aura of the vanished world that made it.

(ii) THE RIVERSIDE
The conservation area of Richmond Riverside, relaxed and

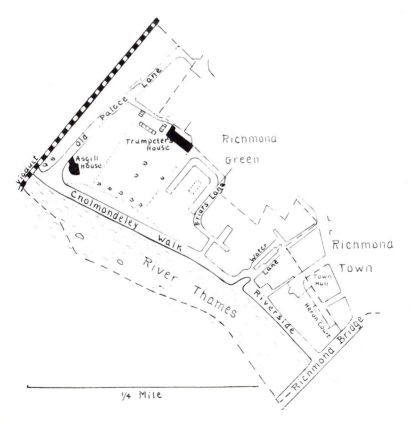

beautiful beside the River Thames, adjoins that of Richmond Green and shares much common history with it. Centuries ago, it too formed part of the tiny village of Richmond where life was focused on the gleaming Tudor palace, with its unusual façade and walls that came down to the water's edge. (The Tudor sovereigns used to travel up to Westminster by river so it was important to have the landing-stage for the State Barge close at hand.)

The stone tablet at the end of Old Palace Lane succinctly highlights some of the early events:

"On this site extending eastward to cloisters of the ancient Friary of Shene stood the river frontage of the Royal Palace, first occupied by Henry I in 1125. Edward I died here in 1377. The Palace was rebuilt by Henry VII who died here in 1509. Queen Elizabeth died here in 1603."

Since those days Richmond Bridge has been built (1774-7) and much water has flowed under it, while the section of the Tudor palace that stood closest to the river has disappeared completely. But the void created by the vanishing palace was filled during the eighteenth century by some notable houses which helped to make this one of the most fashionable places out of London and left the conservation area of today with a special legacy of architectural interest.

The Richmond riverside conservation area stretches from the Twickenham Railway Bridge in the west (where at the end of the seventeenth century Huguenot refugees established one of the first calico works in England) to Richmond Bridge in the east. It includes the ancient ways of Old Palace Lane, Friars Lane and Water Lane, all running at right-angles to the river frontage and linking it, as they always have done, with the green and the old town.

Old Palace Lane near the western boundary is the longest of these ancient thoroughfares but for centuries it remained little more than a rough and muddy track. Before the road was made it was studded with posts and chains, some of which are now used to encircle the grass plot in Old Palace Yard.

By the time Old Palace Lane was improved in 1785, the majestic villa with the pale buff-coloured stone fabric that stands at the river end was already there. Built in 1760, Asgill House was designed by Sir Robert Taylor (designer of the Mansion House in London) as the summer residence of Sir Charles Asgill, a merchant banker who had been Lord Mayor of London in 1757-8. Although this is the smallest of Taylor's villas, it is considered, architecturally, to be his best. Asgill House was enlarged in the 1840s to approximately double its size but in 1969-70 the Victorian additions were removed and the villa now looks much as it did when it was built.

Asgill House

The terrace of small Regency houses about half way up the west side of Old Palace Lane appeared about sixty years after Asgill House. Higher up on the opposite side, Gothic Close (behind a high wall) stands on the site of the old Theatre Royal which was demolished in 1883.

Because of the visual importance of their position, much care was taken over the design of the small new houses in the approach lane to Old Palace Yard. They replaced a row of tiny cottages and stables destroyed in an air-raid during the Second World War.

Although its north-west side faces directly into Old Palace Yard, Trumpeter's House belongs to this conservation area rather than to Richmond Green because its main façade, with portico, eleven bays and great lawn, looks on to the river. A stately home with a tall centre block flanked by two low wings, the house was built early in the eighteenth century for Richard Hill, brother of Mrs Masham, the lady who ousted Sarah Churchill as confidante to Queen Anne. It stands on the site of the Middle Gate of the old Tudor palace and its name – in the past it has also been known as Trumpeting House and Garden Gate House – stems from the fact that it had two stone figures of trumpeters or heralds clad in early Tudor dress standing one on each side of the entrance.

Several distinguished people have lived at Trumpeter's House, including Metternich and Marconi, and it has had many admirers. During a visit to Metternich, Disraeli described it as the most charming house in the world. During the Second World War however, when it was used to accommodate a government department, it became rather dilapidated and it was not until 1952 that it was restored and reorganised internally to form a number of beautifully appointed flats.

Lying a little farther eastward along the river front beyond Queensbury Court (modern flats), Friars Lane forms the dividing line between the site of the old palace and the site of the old friary. Henry VII established the friary alongside his rebuilt palace, roughly where the group of small factories (including the one housed in a converted chapel) and several rows of houses now stand.

Still nearer to Richmond Bridge, steep and narrow Water Lane also has a self-explanatory name – though originally, from 1651 to 1712, it was called Town Lane. The old warehouse at the corner appears in Turner's famous water-colour of Richmond Bridge as an ivory-tinted building, but Water Lane was not really a place noted for sublime and mysterious qualities. As the grooved granite pavements on each side still bear witness, this was where the water-men used to bring their goods-laden carts up from the wharves below and where they used to live in tumbledown hovels or lodging taverns. To most townsfolk it was by no means a popular walk!

However by the nineteenth century most of the river front had turned itself into a fashionable promenade. The part which stretched from Old Palace Lane as far as Water Lane became known as Cholmondeley Walk (after George, the third Earl Cholmondeley) and here, from all accounts, many an animated encounter took place. In the terminology of the day, fashion and beauty from the capital came every summer and mingled with the local quality. In fact the only adverse comment to appear in the records was that less desirable elements such as pickpockets, confidence tricksters and ladies ready to mix business with pleasure had also become aware of its attractions and came up regularly on the steamers.

The row of early eighteenth-century houses known as Heron Court (formerly Herring Court) which stand well back from the river between the end of Water Lane and Richmond Bridge is now scheduled for demolition. The rights and wrongs of demolishing these houses has long been a contentious issue, particularly as the one with the short steep roof that stands in the centre and looks like an old-fashioned doll's house is where Emma Hamilton and her daughter Horatia lived for a time after they left Merton in the years following Nelson's death.

For the most part, however, surprisingly few changes have taken place in recent years to mar the historic and romantic quality of the Richmond Riverside conservation area. With its colourful river activities and splendid view of Richmond Bridge, one can even believe that they never will.

(iii) RICHMOND HILL

Like its neighbours Richmond Green and Richmond Riverside, Richmond Hill ranks as an outstanding conservation area – a distinction it owes in large measure to the legacy of Georgian elegance bequeathed to it by the fashionable ladies and gentlemen of the eighteenth century who came to sample the attractions of the horticultural centre and bracing hillside spa, with its fabulous 'view from the top'.

Although such people have long since vanished from the scene and the clatter of their carriages has been replaced by the noise and congestion of the internal combustion engine, many of the fine houses they occupied still survive and one can still see what *they* saw – the great Thames winding its way serenely through Petersham and Twickenham meadows and, over in the west on a clear day, the towers of Windsor.

The attractions of Richmond Hill may not have been fully appreciated until the eighteenth century but even in the sixteenth century there were a few 'gentlemen's' mansions and a few cottages scattered over the wooded slopes. Two such

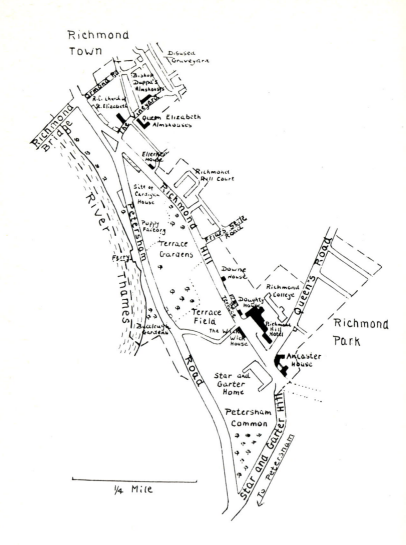

1/4 Mile

cottages, believed to be Elizabethan in origin, are now incorporated into Richmond Gate Hotel (formerly Morshead House). No doubt one of the attractions even in those far-off days was the water supply, for the whole hillside was intersected by streams which trickled down through open ditches and then through leaden pipes into conduits constructed for the benefit of the great palace below.

Nobody knows exactly when the road over the hill appeared but it certainly existed in the seventeenth century, climbing to the summit and then dropping down again into the neighbouring village of Petersham. On the evidence of a seventeenth-century etching, a windmill had also appeared by this time and stood near the summit beside the road.

The conservation area is bounded on its westernmost side by nearly half a mile of river south of Richmond Bridge and takes in the whole of the grassy hillside, with its steep and exhilarating footpaths up to The Terrace and the fine houses that line the old high road still known as Richmond Hill.

Fortunately most of today's heavy traffic is carried by Petersham Road, formerly called the Lower Road, which runs along the river bank and is perhaps best known for its British Legion poppy factory, though one or two eighteenth-century houses still survive here. As this road veers away from the river, it forms a continuation boundary down as far as the southern tip of the small wooded triangular piece of land known as Petersham Common below the Star and Garter Home, all of which is now conservation territory.

If one decides to start at the opposite and more built up northern end of the conservation area, adjacent to the town, there is the added interest of the small complex of streets south and west of the Odeon Cinema, as far as the disused cemetery. Narrow Ormond Road, with its attractive terraced houses built between 1761 and 1778, and the street called The Vineyard, with its Duppa Almshouses, are all included.

The Duppa Almshouses owe their existence to Bishop Brian Duppa who, in 1661, provided for them in his will as a thank-offering for his survival during the Commonwealth. Originally they stood higher up the hill (where Hotel Stuart now stands) and it was not until the middle of the last century that they were rebuilt on the present site using some of the original stone and the whole of the gateway. The Latin inscription on the gateway means: "I will pay the vows which I made to God in my trouble".

No 3 The Terrace

The nearby Queen Elizabeth's Almshouses were founded in 1600 and originally stood in the Lower Road before being rebuilt here in The Vineyard during the 1760s.

As one starts the journey up the hill, it is interesting to note the graceful bow-windowed upper storeys of a few of the shops. These buildings are, of course, converted eighteenth-century houses. They were bought up in the early part of the present century by speculators who recognised the demand for more shopping facilities by people coming up to Richmond from London for a day's outing.

The current demand for homes rather than for shops accounts for the large blocks of flats which, in recent times, have replaced many of the large villas that once graced this famous hillside. Terrace Gardens, however, still basks in the immunity bestowed on it nearly a hundred years ago. The gardens were created in the middle of the last century by Walter Montague Douglas-Scott who lived at Buccleuch House in Petersham Road but in 1886 this precious piece of land with the magnificent view came suddenly on the market and was about to be bought up by speculators for the building of "desirable villas". Fortunately the vestry of the day became alerted to the danger and, despite vigorous protests from the ratepayers, made the bold decision to purchase the land for the benefit of the town. Ever since that day it has been public property.

Until recently, eighteenth-century Cardigan House, once owned by the fifth Earl of Cardigan, forbear of the seventh earl who led the Six Hundred at Balaclava, stood at the beginning of Terrace Walk. Despite its Grade 2 classification, Cardigan House with its large Venetian window, was demolished in 1971 to make way for British Legion flats and the redevelopment of the Poppy Factory. Originally its garden reached right down to the river.

With its castellated exterior, Ellerker House (No 48) on the opposite side of the road dates back to the early eighteenth century when it was occupied by the widow and daughter of Sir John Houblon, first Governor of the Bank of England. Beneath the cement facing is a red-brick house. It became a school in 1889.

Higher up, on the brow of the hill beyond Friars Stile Road, eighteenth-century Downe House (now Nos 114-118) has the distinction of having been leased by R.S. Sheridan for several years from about 1806.

From their even more elevated position, several of the houses of The Terrace also had distinguished occupants – perhaps none more so than No 3. This small and narrow house, one of the finest in Richmond, was built about 1760, probably by Sir Robert Taylor, for George III's card maker and it is believed that Mrs Fitzherbert lived here at the time she met the twenty-year old future George IV, then Prince of Wales. Following their secret marriage by the Vicar of Twickenham in 1785, the couple spent their honeymoon at No 3 and no doubt often looked down over the broad steeply sloping field to what is now Petersham Road beside the river.

The house at the top of steep Nightingale Lane which skirts the sloping field is 'The Wick'. Designed by Robert Mylne in 1775 and now considered a perfect Georgian house, it stands on the site of the old Bull's Head Inn.

The Wick

Wick House next door was built about three years earlier, between 1769 and 1772, by Sir William Chambers. Designed specially as a weekend home of Sir Joshua Reynolds, it was from its windows that the artist painted his famous *Petersham and Twickenham Meadows*. In the days of Reynolds' occupation, Wick House was used to entertain many leading figures of the literary world, including Dr Johnson, James Boswell, Edmund Burke and Oliver Goldsmith, but after Reynolds' death a subsequent owner encased it in stucco and it lost its original appearance. It was restored during the 1950s for use as an annexe for staff of the Star and Garter Home for Disabled Soldiers, Sailors and Airmen.

Standing across the road from The Wick, Doughty House was originally a mid-eighteenth-century mansion built for Henry Doughty and lived in for many years by his daughter Elizabeth, a pious Roman Catholic, who was responsible for the building of St Elizabeth Church in The Vineyard. In 1849 this house was bought by the art collector Francis Cook and housed one of the finest collections of Old Masters in the country. In the late 1880s, however, Doughty House was Victorianised and has now been turned into flats. (The last of the Cook Collection was sold in 1965, mostly to U.S. galleries.)

The Richmond Gate Hotel now incorporates several eighteenth-century houses – Marsfield House, Crawford

Cottage, The Cottage, Syon House and Morshead House – and is listed Grade Two. It was here, or very close to here, that the windmill shown on various seventeenth-century maps, once stood.

The large Perpendicular building of Bath stone which stands behind the hotel, with access from Queen's Road, is Richmond College, built in the years 1841 to 1843 as a training centre for Methodist ministers. In 1975 however it became an American Institute for Foreign Study.

The conservation area also takes in a further short stretch of Queen's Road so as to include the enclave of four cul-de-sacs on its opposite (east) side just beyond the public house which calls itself 'The Lass of Richmond Hill'. The identity of Richmond's 'lass' remains something of a mystery. There have been claims and counter claims about who she was and where she lived, but so far nobody has convincingly established either her name or that of the poet who so fervently sang her praises.

The large building at the corner of Queen's Road and Richmond Park's main entrance is Ancaster House. It was built in 1772 for Peregrine, Duke of Ancaster on the site of a hunting lodge but it soon passed into the hands of Sir Lionel Darell who was a friend of George III. The story has it that during a casual encounter with the king in the park, Darell mentioned that he wanted to build more greenhouses but did not have enough land, whereupon the king immediately presented him with an extra plot. The house now serves as the official residence of the Commandant of the Star and Garter Home and also houses some of the nursing staff.

Since it was built shortly after the end of the First World War, the Star and Garter Home has remained in command at the top of Richmond Hill. It stands on the site of two successive Star and Garter hotels, the first of which was started in 1738 as a humble inn devoid even of accommodation for overnight travellers. Gradually however the eighteenth-century inn expanded and finally rose to stardom under ever increasing patronage from royalty, poets, politicians and novelists. A few writers, including Thackeray in *Vanity Fair*, even used it as a story setting for some of their novels and understandably there was much dismay when, in 1870, it was destroyed by fire.

The second Star and Garter Hotel, built to replace the old, was not a success. It was far too big and had none of the old atmosphere, with the result that it quickly degenerated into what became popularly known as the 'white elephant' of Richmond Hill. So, in 1919, after a relatively short life, the 'white elephant' had to go, leaving the site free for the construction of the home for disabled war veterans.

If one stands at the top of Richmond Hill away from the traffic and looks down upon this exhilarating conservation area, it is certainly not difficult to understand the thinking that lay behind the 1919 decision. If any view was to convince the wounded that England had been worth fighting for, surely this was it.

18

Strand-on-the-Green

Waterfront

Looking more like an eighteenth-century fishing village – which is what it used to be – than a London suburb, Strand-on-the-Green stretches out from below Kew Bridge for a distance of some three-quarters of a mile downstream in the direction of Hammersmith and London. The conservation area covers the whole waterfront, with its long continuous row of attractive old houses, cottages and inns backing on to Thames Street, plus a little of the hinterland.

Unlike the neighbouring conservation area of old Chiswick beyond Duke's Meadows, this unspoilt waterside colony possesses no important buildings, and never has done. In fact until about 1770 when a few larger but unpretentious houses

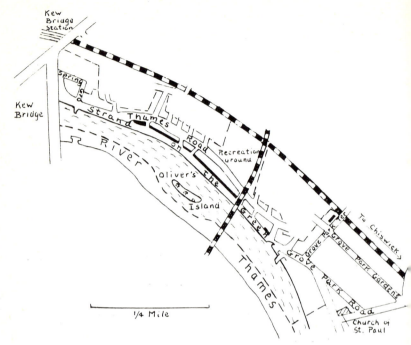

began to appear, it consisted of little more than fishermen's cottages and understandably became known as Chiswick's second village.

Although the Brentford tower blocks just west of Kew Bridge are now a permanent feature of the skyline, reminding one how times have changed since those days, it is interesting to see how much Strand-on-the-Green has retained its old immunity to the engulfing pressures of the capital. The most popular theory to explain the phenomenon is of course the river itself and the physical limitations imposed by it.

At the same time Strand-on-the-Green probably owes its existence to the river – as indeed the name itself suggests. Strond or Stronde, as the hamlet was originally called, means 'bordering a river'.

Not much is known about the hamlet's early history but if one starts at the pleasant little area at the Kew Bridge end of the conservation area where there are plenty of seats from which to contemplate the passing boats, the strong reflected light on the water and the unrestricted view eastward, it is

almost impossible to believe that its attractions passed down
the centuries unnoticed. In fact there are plenty of indications
that, like Kew on the opposite bank, this was once a British
settlement with the traditional complement no doubt of
primitive riverside huts. Over the years the river bed between
Kew and Hammersmith has yielded a copious supply of small
relics of flint, stone and metal, many of them weapons of war
of the pre-Roman period. The story of the hamlet's
subsequent development was mostly unrecorded but it is
known that it eventually acquired a village green and
common, both of which disappeared a century or more ago.

Even if the pleasures of setting out along the narrow traffic-
free riverside 'street', with its overhanging willows,
nineteenth-century lamp posts and gleaming houses, are
tempered by a few initial misgivings about the almost
complete absence of protective railings, there is, according to
those who live here, no need to worry! Although the
waterfront comes literally up to within two or three yards of
people's front doors, no one it seems – at least not in recent
times – has actually fallen into the water. Hence when safety
was put forward a few years ago by the local authority as a
reason for replacing the old lamp posts by new concrete ones,
the proposal was successfully defeated. The inhabitants of
Strand-on-the-Green made it plain that they preferred their
old lamp posts, so now, suitably electrified and protected by a
preservation order, these decorative relics of gaslight days
have acquired a new lease of life.

Haphazard yet curiously harmonious, many of the houses
and cottages along the waterfront were built in the eighteenth
and early nineteenth centuries and are also on the grade two
scheduled list. It is thought that the large white stuccoed
house, No 70 Strand-on-the-Green, with the protruding
balconies and red brick doorway with elliptical arch, may
once have been the residence of the mariner Zachary, famous
for his feat of swimming twenty-two leagues from one island to
another with a tinder box and matches wrapped dry in his
hair. The house was refronted with stucco during the
nineteenth century and more recently some of its three-
storeyed neighbours, including Carlton House and No 67,
followed suit. The latter were all built in the eighteenth
century.

No 65 Strand-on-the-Green, easily recognised by the small
recumbent terracotta lion over the front doorway, was, as its

blue plaque proclaims, once the home of the artist Zoffany. Now known as Zoffany House, it was commenced about 1704 and was occupied by the artist for twenty years, from 1790 to 1810. Born in Frankfurt in 1733, Johann Zoffany had come to England as a struggling artist and almost starved in a Drury Lane garret before achieving recognition and success, chiefly as a society and royal portrait painter, though his real talent lay in dramatic scenes and conversation pieces. It was after his return from India, where he earned a lot of money at the court of an Indian ruler, that Zoffany settled down in Strand-on-the-Green and, despite impaired powers, went on painting. For his picture of *The Last Supper*, now in St Paul's Church, Brentford, he used local fishermen as models for eleven of the apostles and himself as the model for St Peter. When he died in 1810, leaving four daughters by his second marriage, he was buried in Kew churchyard just across the river.

The house next door called Magnolia House (No 64) belongs to the early nineteenth century but just beyond this three-storeyed group, quaint little Compass House (No 61), with its front door perched on high at the top of nine steps, was probably built a little earlier, as was No 56. It was close to this spot that a shambling old malt house, visible in many an old photograph, stood until it was demolished early this century.

The carefully designed terrace of white brick, three-storeyed houses numbered 52 to 55, with Oliver House in the middle, belongs to the early nineteenth century – a little later than the two-storeyed red brick No 50 with its old tiled hipped roof just beyond. No 49, conspicuous by its half-sized door suitable only for midgets at the top of the two white painted stone steps, also belongs to the early nineteenth century.

Of mid-nineteenth-century vintage, the pair of white painted houses numbered 46 and 47 originally formed a malthouse and warehouse. Hence the large double doors flush with the brickwork and the ornamental window grilles. Beyond it, built in brown brick, both Picton House (No 45) with its traceried fanlight, and Wisteria House (No 44) living up to its name with its delightful wall creeper, belong to the eighteenth century.

There was much dismay in Strand-on-the-Green when the adjoining site, now occupied by the elevated terrace of four new red brick houses, was relinquished by the Port of London Authority. For years this site had been used as a repair yard, its coils of rope, drums of tar and other nautical impedimenta adding their own touch of interest and colour to the riverside scene. The first proposal for redevelopment was for tall high density houses but this at least was successfully opposed by the Strand-on-the-Green Association. The older bay-windowed terrace with white-painted weather-boarding, known as 'Magnolia Wharf', also stands on the site of a former barge repairing workshop.

The public house called 'The City Barge' which stands beside narrow Post Office Alley was so named because the Lord Mayor's barge used to be moored here in winter. There was in fact a series of such barges, the most remarkable of which was the *Maria Wood* built in 1816 at a cost of £3000. As shown in an old print, this 136-foot long vessel was painted blue with gold relief and it is said to have been capable of carrying two hundred persons on its upper deck. The Lord Mayor and aldermen used to come here to embark before being towed upstream by horses, often as far as Hampton Court or Staines.

The 'Bull's Head' was built in the eighteenth century, probably on the site of a sixteenth-century inn, about the same time as the two brown brick houses which separate it from the 'City Barge'. The tradition that Oliver Cromwell held a military court at the old inn is unconfirmed but at least it seems likely that the eighteenth-century comic actor Joe Miller, one of the village's best known inhabitants, was among its early patrons. Miller is remembered because, although unable to read – he had to rely on his wife when learning his lines – he played as many as fifty-nine parts from the plays of Shakespeare and the Restoration dramatists.

If its early patrons came back today, no doubt they would find the white-painted inn, with its modern ground-floor addition, greatly changed but they might still recognise the old tree-covered landmark just offshore – Oliver's Island.

Oliver's Island is now part of the conservation area which means that any development or other claims by aspiring occupants, including one in recent times by a pop group, are likely to be resisted. In this respect the island is now probably better off than it was in 1796 when, in the words of one report, it was "ornamented with a wooden building in the shape of a castle". The 'castle' was the home of the Thames Committee who also owned a barge – "a very large and curious vessel fitted up as a habitation for those persons appointed to receive tolls ... to pay the interest of the loan raised to improve the navigation of this part of the river".

The need for improved navigation was, however, only one of many problems of which Strand-on-the-Green was made aware during the nineteenth century. Pollution was now the major enemy, killing off virtually all the fish and depriving the fishermen of a living. Although eventually, by the second half of the present century, the Thames had been made cleaner, it was too late to bring back the old fishermen and when the lamprey and small eel, once very numerous along this stretch of water, began to reappear there was only the amateur angler to appreciate the catch!

In addition to angling, sailing has become one of Strand-on-the-Green's leisure activities and in the summer a sailing club operates from beneath the onshore arches of the high and massive railway bridge which so prominently spans the river just east of Oliver's Island. Hence the numerous small craft one sees moored and afloat.

The bridge itself still arouses a variety of reactions. When it was built about 1867 to a design by W.R. Galbraith to link Gunnersbury and Kew Gardens stations, Zoffany's successors, who still lived on the waterfront, were far from appreciative. Attitudes however have since mellowed and today the stalwart iron structure, now a familiar part of the landscape, has many admirers.

A few years ago, despite the increasing interest in Strand-on-the-Green's historical and architectural past, several old waterside cottages were threatened with demolition when leases ran out and the brewery decided to sell off some of its property. The two cottages now successfully incorporated into the 'Bull's Head' were part of this group and were only saved from extinction by the efforts of local residents who, through their Association, mounted an energetic rescue operation. Also rescued were Nos 10, 11 and 12, all now refurbished and repaired to form the three residences jointly known as Bull Cottage.

Even luckier, one might say, was the group of cottage almshouses which stands just beyond this point at right angles to the river, for here the first escape came earlier in the century before the age of conservation. Dating back to 1704, the almshouses were founded "for the use of the Poor of Chiswick for Ever" but despite this optimistic message to posterity, they came up for sale in 1931 and only narrowly survived through the generosity of Mr B. Hopkin-Morris after whom they were re-named. The second deliverance came in 1972 when, after much deliberation, the local authority finally agreed to provide them with modern amenities and to restore the frontages' original features which had not been preserved in 1933.

The balconied house with the central bay, now known as Strand-on-the-Green House but formerly called 'The Elms', which brings one to the end of this delightful riverside walk, was built, like its somewhat altered neighbours Nos 2 and 3, in the eighteenth century.

Although at this point one has to begin retreating from the waterfront into Thames Street, the conservation area continues along the river bank past the small jetty for another hundred yards or so. It also takes in most of the residential area behind this stretch of river – the area bounded by Grove Park Road and Grove Park Terrace as far as the railway line.

These attractive tree-lined streets – Grove Park Road with its mixture of late Victorian and early twentieth-century houses, Grove Park Avenue with its Edwardian villas and Grove Park Terrace with its group of Georgian houses near the level crossing – clearly reflect the various stages of expansion which eventually overtook the tiny fishing village. The church of St Paul at the eastern corner of Grove Park Road was built in 1872 to serve the growing population but it had to be extensively repaired as a result of war damage.

If one returns to Kew Bridge along Thames Street, with its shops on one side and occasional alleyways giving sudden glimpses of the river between walled-in gardens on the other, one may wonder yet again how two quite different worlds have managed to co-exist for so long. With the roar of main road traffic growing louder and the Brentford tower blocks looming taller, is it really true that an old waterfront so close to London town still retains so much of its old identity?

19

Twickenham – Riverside

Eel Pie Island Bridge

In the eighteenth century the three-quarter mile stretch of Thamesside facing Eel Pie Island lay at the centre of the long straggling and irregular village of Twickenham and was noted both for its sylvan beauty and for its elegance and desirability as a place to live. Since those days modern suburbia has taken over nearly all the surrounding land, yet miraculously this nucleus remains almost intact – and probably almost as scenic.

To reach it, all one has to do is detach oneself from busy King Street or York Street and saunter down one of the narrow streets leading to the river. The conservation area, which includes the offshore island, extends from Wharf Lane on the west to Montpelier Row just beyond Orleans Park on the east.

Since Twickenham grew up around the church, perhaps this is as good a place as any to start. Recent excavations have shown that in prehistoric times a habitation existed near by, though the earliest documentary reference to the village was in the year 704 when the King of the East Saxons granted a piece

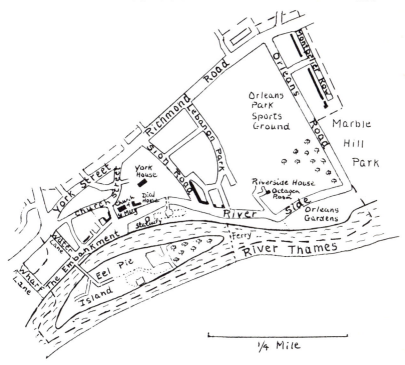

of land at Tuican-hom in the province of Middel Seaxon.

Later Twickenham won a brief mention in the Domesday Book – it was then part of the manor of Isleworth in the Hundred of Hounslow – but for the most part this fascinating village appears to have passed through the centuries curiously devoid of incident. In fact somebody once said that it was one of those happy places not burdened with a history.

Another of Twickenham's recorded peculiarities is its eighteenth-century reputation for being the most untittle-tattling village in the country – despite the fact that most of its leading inhabitants at that time were dowagers!

The church dates mainly from 1714, when most of it was rebuilt following the collapse of the nave one April night in 1713. If the present roomy, red-brick structure built in the so-called Tuscan style to the design of John James, architect of St George's, Hanover Square, appears rather out of keeping with the battlemented fourteenth-century tower to which it remains joined, at least the architectural mistake is amply compensated for by its delightful situation.

Among the interesting monuments in Twickenham Church is the one on the east wall of the north gallery erected by Alexander Pope to his parents. This early eighteenth-century poet and wit, who translated the *Iliad* but spent so much of his time laying elaborate plots for the deception of posterity and his contemporaries alike, lived only half a mile away, at Cross Deep, in the celebrated Pope's Villa (now demolished), with its fantastic grotto under the road. Having brought so much fame to Twickenham, Pope was buried in 1744 in a vault beneath the floor of the nave, near the chancel step.

In the early days an ancient manor house, reputedly the dower house of Henry VIII's first wife, Catherine of Aragon, stood opposite the church gates on the north side of Church Street. Eventually however this was replaced by a large red brick mansion called Aragon Towers which, together with the nearby old Sawyer's Inn, was demolished a few years ago, amid a storm of protest, to make way for a proposed Civic Centre with three hundred car parking spaces. So far the controversial redevelopment has not materialised but if it ever does it would mean the demolition of several more old properties. The existing car park on the south side of Church Street, created after a group of eighteenth-century cottages were demolished in 1960, is included in the redevelopment plans. So too are the school buildings in School Alley erected in 1809.

The existing group of cottages, some with frontages in Church Lane, others round the corner into The Embankment, owe their survival partly to the intervention of Sir John Betjeman who was called on to help resist the demolition plan. Nearly all the survivors, including Nos 22 and 23 The Embankment tucked away in their narrow cul-de-sac, were built about 1720. The fire insurance plate on the wall of No 22 bears witness to the age to which they belonged.

The more substantial red brick houses at the western (Bell Lane) end of this interesting old thoroughfare that runs parallel with the river, including Strand House and No 2 The Embankment, were built about the same time, early in the eighteenth century. Bell House in Bell Lane, which forms part of The Embankment block, was originally the back wing of No 1 The Embankment. It took the name of a house which, until demolished by a bomb, stood on the opposite side of the lane.

The Embankment

Fortunately neither bombs nor redevelopment schemes appear to have dispelled the delightful holiday-like air which pervades this most scenic of conservation areas. Crowds come every summer to watch or take part in the boating activities which extend all along the embankment from the end of Church Lane, thereby adding to a scene more reminiscent of a seaside harbour than a London suburb.

At present the narrow iron foot-bridge opposite the end of Water Lane and the 'Barmy Arms' (with its 'barmy' upside-down inn sign) provides the residents of Eel Pie Island with their only means of access. Much of the 530-yard long islet or eyot has become the private property of the owners of the small houses, bungalows, boat-building yard and rowing club now established there.

For centuries Eel Pie Island was a favourite resort of Thames anglers, boating parties and excursionists and it was for their accommodation that a small and unassuming barn-like inn called Eel Pie House, celebrated for its eel pies, came into existence. This old inn on the south-east side was pulled down in 1830 and replaced by the larger Eel Pie Tavern, but now that too has gone. Some years ago the site was acquired by a building firm and, after changing hands, was finally redeveloped with blocks of town houses in white brick. Despite the presence of the bird sanctuary close by, this led to proposals for the creation of a new bridge from the Surrey side wide enough to take motor traffic. So far however Eel Pie Island remains the preserve of pedestrians.

Back on shore, the long leafy lane called Riverside, which starts at the bottom of Church Lane and takes one the whole way to the conservation area's eastern boundary with Marble Hill Park, used to be a great favourite with Twickenham's eighteenth-century inhabitants. The only thing that worried them was the flooding hazard and it was for this reason that so many of the houses were built in streets leading off from the river at right angles in the direction of the main Richmond Road rather than along the embankment itself. The high water level of the river floods of 1774, still clearly marked on the high wall at the corner of Riverside and Church Lane, was obviously something of more than academic interest.

The long yellow brick vicarage which comes into view as soon as the lane narrows between the enclosing high walls of York House Gardens is still known as Dial House because of its tall rectangular sundial (1726) above the front entrance. The house itself however is Victorian. It was built in 1896 by Thomas Twining, founder of the well-known firm of London tea merchants, who was no doubt unaware that before long his upper windows would enjoy a commanding view of the back of 'Venus', the presiding central figure in the remarkable group of elevated statuary erected by Sir Ratan Tata, last private owner of York House in the beautiful riverside gardens across the road.

If one reserves the close-up view of this prodigious piece of work for the return journey and continues along Riverside under the hump-backed stone bridge which links the two parts of York House Gardens, the scene soon reverts back to the more sombre splendour of the eighteenth century. Sion Row is believed to have been built in 1721 and, apart from Sion Cottage (1854) at the corner, most of the houses facing Riverside between the end of Sion Road and Lebanon Grove were built in the same century. Several of them, however, including the White Swan Inn with its balustraded terrace, have suffered from later alterations and additions.

It is interesting to see that the ancient Twickenham ferry still functions, providing those who want to cross the river with a spasmodic but useful service and the romantically minded with a scene reminiscent of one of those ancient ballads about eloping couples chased by irate or disapproving fathers who finally and sometimes tragically catch up with their quarry at the water's edge.

But, as the great house just around the corner – or what remains of a great house – bears witness, the days of rank and wealth associated with such romantic adventures have gone. Now reduced to little more than the Octagon Room, interesting example of James Gibbs' baroque though this is, Orleans House is now only a shadow of the mansion it once was. The days when Louis Philippe of France (in 1800) and later Don Carlos of Spain (in 1876) made it their home are a thing of the past. Complete with wooded grounds and the adjacent Riverside House, Orleans House was bequeathed by its late owner to the local authority who eventually turned it into the municipal art gallery it is today.

The Octagon Room of Orleans House

On the north side, the land known as the Orleans Sports Ground was also once part of this estate and so was the fine stretch of riverside gardens, both of which now form part of the conservation area.

The conservation area's eastern boundary follows Orleans Road northward as far as the White Cottage and then veers a little to the east so as to take in the splendid eighteenth-century Montpelier Row. Many of the attractive colour-washed cottages, with their numerous window boxes, at the upper end of Orleans Road were originally mews cottages attached to the fine houses of Montpelier Row.

Not surprisingly several successful poets and writers of the last century were attracted to this part of Twickenham. As the plaque on No 15 Montpelier Row proclaims, this large house on the corner of the lane (Chapel Road) which links the two roads was the home of Lord Tennyson while South End House (No 30), still with its square brick gazebo in the grounds looking towards the river, was where Walter de la Mare lived during the later years of his life.

The northern boundary of the conservation area has been slightly extended in recent times but it roughly follows Richmond Road and its continuation York Street. Busy York Street takes its name of course from York House whose origins date back to the fifteenth and sixteenth centuries when it was known as Yorke's Farm. In 1661 York House was granted to the son and heir of the Earl of Clarendon and later passed to his brother the Earl of Rochester. There followed a long list of distinguished residents until eventually, in the mid-1920s, the enlarged brick mansion was sold to the local authority.

Sir Ratan Tata, who was the last private owner of the seven-acre York House estate with its fine trees and gardens extending as far as the river, was an Indian merchant prince and wealthy industrialist. He was knighted in 1916 and among his various philanthropic activities was his foundation of the Ratan Tata Department of Social Sciences at the London School of Economics. But as far as Twickenham is concerned, the most memorable act of this colourful figure was undoubtedly the erection of the waterfall statuary which continues to surprise unsuspecting visitors to the gardens as they emerge from the labyrinth of little paths and yew shrubberies centred upon the Round Pond.

With its elevated Venus-like figure poised on a high rock between two rearing horses and its seven stone maidens in extraordinary postures reaching up towards her, the statuary has been variously claimed to represent the birth of Venus or the pearl fishers. So far no one has offered any prizes either for interpretation or for artistic rating, but neither has anyone denied that the massive stone composition makes its own unique contribution to the character of this outstanding conservation area.

20

Wimbledon Village

Corner of High Street and Church Road

Even today a breath of heathland is in one's nostrils as one enters Wimbledon village at the end of the long high road from Putney. Although still a law unto itself and not part of the Wimbledon village conservation area, the famous common, once the haunt of highwaymen and scene of many a celebrated duel, is clearly a dominating influence.

Flanked by its cluster of attractive houses and standing at the south-east corner of the common just beyond the war memorial, the triangular green marks the beginning of the High Street section of the conservation area and also provides a distant glimpse across Rushmere Pond of the eighteenth- and nineteenth-century mansions of West Side. West Side serves as a boundary for a larger section of designated territory extending as far west as the ancient earthwork known since 1800 as Caesar's Camp.

Despite the name given to this earthwork, there is no historical evidence to suggest that Julius Caesar or any other Roman ever set foot on Wimbledon's dry and open hill top. It is known that in Saxon times there was a small farming settlement here and the name of Wimbledon is thought to be derived from the Anglo-Saxon 'dun' meaning 'hill' added to a proper name such as Wynnman. In other words, this could have been Wynnman's Hill.

Apart from the name and the discovery of some traces of an early British habitation (probably about 300 BC), little is known about Wimbledon's ancient past. In fact, as part of the old manor of Mortlake, the hamlet did not even get a mention in the Domesday Book. Nevertheless there are indications that a medieval village existed here and it only needed Thomas Cecil in 1588 to recognise its advantages as an attractive place to live and to set about building Wimbledon House, an elaborate and stately mansion, on the distant slopes of the hill (astride what is now Home Park Road) to turn it into a place of importance.

Although Wimbledon House and the mansions that succeeded it were all destined to have relatively short lives, the village itself continued to be a favourite resort of London's upper classes and by the eighteenth century it had a growing colony of large exclusive residences bordering the southern tip of the common. At least part of this colony survived the arrival in 1838 of the railway, with its accompanying influx of commuters (at first mainly those who could afford to rent or buy houses or land on the virgin slopes leading up to the top of the hill) and the large scale middle class invasion that followed. In fact, together with the old High Street, it now accounts for much of the Wimbledon village conservation area.

If one approaches the High Street from the green, it is easy enough to visualise the nineteenth-century village as it used to be. The square and solid looking inn called the 'Rose and Crown' on the north side of the road was once the chief tavern and was where the vestry meetings were often held. It was also a haunt of writers, notably of Leigh Hunt and Swinburne, and was the starting point for coaches to London via Putney. The inn was built in the seventeenth century and is known to have had a bowling alley as early as 1670.

Set well back from the road just beyond the 'Rose and Crown', the splendid though much altered Jacobean house

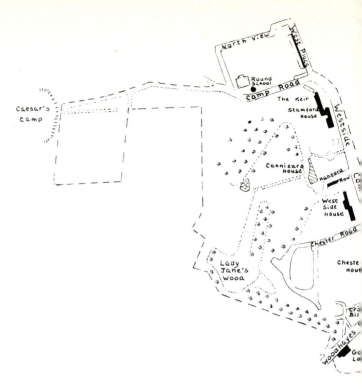

with the three gables and central oriel window was once among the most important in Wimbledon – as indeed, from the architectural point of view, it still is. Built in 1613 of red brick (since rendered over) by Robert Bell of the East India Company, it had several well-known owners, including the Marquis of Bath and Pitt's foreign minister William Grenville. At the beginning of the nineteenth century, Eagle House, as it is now called, was turned into a school by the Reverend Thomas Lancaster, Vicar of Merton, who named it Nelson House after his illustrious parishioner Lord Nelson. This name however was soon superseded by the present one when a new owner, a Dr Huntingford, arrived in 1860 bringing with him a stone eagle which he erected prominently on top of the central gable.

In 1887 Eagle House was in a poor way and about to be demolished for redevelopment purposes when the architect Sir Thomas Jackson bought it. Jackson, who had studied under Sir Gilbert Scott, removed the old school annexe and restored the house for use as a private residence. Today the house is

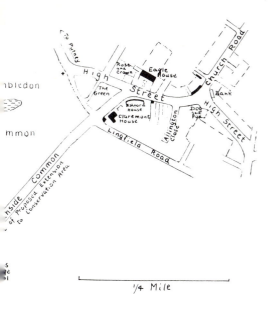

used as offices but the coats of arms and initials which stand above the main door are preserved as reminders of its two important occupants: RB REGN IACI (Robert Bell in the reign of James I) and JGJ REGN VICT (Thomas Graham Jackson in the reign of Queen Victoria).

The row of shops just beyond Eagle House on this side of the High Street are nearly all converted from very old properties but the double-fronted tile-hung group with the imposing central bell tower where the road begins to swing round into Church Road was originally the old fire station built in 1890. It was because of this building's prominent corner position that its wall was chosen as the site for the bronze plaque recording the Civic Trust award received by the village in 1968 for its High Street improvements.

Round the corner in Church Road, the pair of tile-hung cottages with a shop and restaurant on the ground floors date from the late seventeenth century and are among the village's earliest surviving buildings.

The conservation area extends along Church Road past the

Eagle House

long row of nineteenth-century shops and cottages as far as Lancaster Road where nineteenth-century Rose Cottage, used last century as an armoury for volunteer soldiers, stands at the corner. Tucked away in the cul-de-sac near the High Street end of Church Road, Walnut Tree Cottages date back to the eighteenth century, whereas those in Belvedere Square on the opposite side of the road are Victorian.

As one turns back from Church Road and rounds the corner to resume the journey south-eastwards along the High Street, it is interesting to note how important the bank was in those expansionist days of a hundred years ago. Looking more like a French *château* than a repository for people's money, the tall dominating terracotta building on the corner must have impressed many a newcomer and potential customer.

The extra width and slight change of direction of the High Street at this point puzzles some people but it has a natural explanation. It was here that one of the traditional enclosures for stray animals once stood, close to the stocks and 'cage'. As time went on these disappeared but the open space found alternative uses and towards the end of the last century, before it became a busy traffic junction, it was a well-known venue for performances by travelling players.

With its open view across the traffic island to Church Road, the 'Dog and Fox' is a relatively modern building but it stands on a site where inns – the seventeenth-century one was called

'My Lord's Inn' – have stood for at least four hundred years.

East of the 'Dog and Fox', the shop-lined stretch of High Street extending as far as the Ridgway completes this end of the conservation area. Unlike the rest of the High Street leading back to the green which constitutes the original village, it was built in Victorian times.

The oldest and most interesting part of the village is undoubtedly the stretch of High Street between the 'Dog and Fox' and the green. There is good reason to believe that here, on the south side of the street, a row of medieval cottages and farms once stood – a theory strongly supported by the long regular plots of land which one can just see through some of the arches between the shops and which show up clearly on the map. It is now believed that these plots were once strips of common field.

No one is sure when the old farmhouses disappeared but, apart from the tenements of Allington Close built in 1872 by Lord Spencer, Lord of the Manor, most of the buildings which now line this side of the High Street, including the stretch which sweeps round towards the common, date back to the seventeenth and eighteenth century. No 35, now used as a doctor's surgery, was built in 1760. The shop fronts were added when the Victorian and Edwardian expansion began.

The largest of these converted buildings, standing on the inner bend opposite the large furniture store (site of Wimbledon's first post office), is Ashford House. Although extended and altered when the Victorian shop fronts were added, Ashford House is still basically the building put up in 1720 as a private house. There have been various attempts over the years to have it demolished but now it is a listed property.

Its immediate neighbour, built as a bakery, stands on the site of the original village smithy which remained a familiar sight for hundreds of years right up to the end of the last century. The pair of large stone lions which adorn the front entrance of the adjoining house, No 41 High Street, are all that is left of an old house called Wimbledon Villa built in 1797 on Southside overlooking the common.

The disappearance from Southside of this and similar houses, including Lauriston House where William Wilberforce once lived (the converted stable block remains), accounts for the non-designated area between the High Street part of the conservation area and the more westerly part. An extension of the boundaries is under consideration but at present attractive L-shaped Claremont House, built in the late seventeenth century, possibly on the site of an older house, and its neighbour No 45, completes the High Street section. *

The larger more westerly section begins with the buildings of King's College School – a boys' public school transferred here in 1897 from the Strand where it had begun life as the Junior Department of King's College, London. The simple white Georgian house with Doric porch which the school took over had been built in 1750 and in 1899 this was extended to include the Great Hall built in Gothic Revival style by Sir Banister Fletcher. A relic of those days is the Penfold hexagonal pillar box on the pavement outside which has now served this corner of the village for more than a hundred years.

Standing just beyond Wright's Alley where Southside merges into Woodhayes Road, Southside House was owned for many years by the physician and writer Axel Munthe and became somewhat neglected during his absence abroad. However it is now occupied by his son and the School Teachers Cultural Foundation. The interesting and attractive façade was built in 1687, though there is a trace of an earlier building in the clock tower. The wrought iron work over the small entrance gate records that the house was extended and altered in 1776, a date which coincides with the two fire insurance plates at the front.

Farther down in the hollow of the road, the romantic looking white walled house with Tudor windows on the ground floor and ogee-arched windows above is Gothic Lodge. Built in 1763 at a time when Gothic Revival architecture was becoming popular, Gothic Lodge had several occupants with literary connections. There was Lady Anne Barnard, author of the Scottish ballad *Auld Robin Gray* and, later on, about 1820, the novelist-explorer Captain Frederick Marryat who used it as a temporary home while writing some of his sea tales.

Standing behind the triangular grass plots on the opposite side of the road, the two inns known as the 'Crooked Billet' and the 'Hand in Hand' are seventeenth century in origin but both have been much altered.

The mansion called Chester House at the south corner of Westside looking towards Rushmere Pond, now with a small well laid out council estate at its rear, was built about 1670 and was once the home of Pitt's great rival, John Horne

* Since this book went to press, the conservation area has been extended.

Gothic Lodge

Tooke. Tooke was a man who wanted to devote his life to radical politics but, despite an eventual election success at Old Sarum, he was refused a seat in parliament because he had been ordained. Although he built a tomb for himself in his back garden, his executors decided that the proper place for him was in Ealing churchyard and acted accordingly. With its modern addition, the house is now used as a training centre for Barclays Bank.

Now regarded as a shadow of its former self, West Side House a little farther along was built about 1760. Among its various occupants was Lord Lyndhurst, an early nineteenth-century lord chancellor. Later on it became the home of the second Viscount Melville. No doubt many of its early occupants benefited from the services of the artisans of the six cottages called Hanford Row which stands close by at the end of a short private road. As the wall inscription on the little terrace proclaims, Hanford Row was built in 1770.

The large and conspicuous building with the dual carriageway just beyond is Cannizaro House, now used as an old people's home. It is a rebuilt version of an eighteenth-century mansion which was almost completely destroyed by fire in 1900. The name derives from the Duke of Cannizaro, an impoverished Sicilian who married an English heiress in 1806 and took up residence with her here for a few years – until the attractions of a Milanese beauty summoned him back to his native land. Earlier occupants included Lyde Brown(e), Governor of the Bank of England, who is said to have died of apoplexy when the Empress of Russia paid him only half of what she owed him for a remarkable collection of Greek and Roman antiquities (now a major part of the central collection in the Hermitage, Leningrad). There was also Henry Dundas who became Viscount Melville in 1786.

It was Viscount Melville who laid out the splendid park, including Lady Jane's Wood which he planted in honour of Lady Jane Hope whom he eventually married in 1793 after having waited two years in vain for a favourable sign from his absent neighbour Lady Anne Lindsay, later Lady Anne Barnard of Gothic Lodge. Over a century later, during the First World War, the rebuilt house was used as a convalescent home for officers and was later acquired by Edward Kenneth Wilson who also bought the neighbouring house The Keir for conversion into flats, using part of the grounds to extend his Cannizaro estate. In 1948 Mr Wilson's daughter sold the whole of Cannizaro to the Wimbledon Corporation for £40,000 and the park was opened to the public.

Just beyond the entrance to Cannizaro Park, No 22A West Side stands on the site of the old Sun Ale House – an inn closed at the end of the eighteenth century on grounds of riotous behaviour. Until the site was redeveloped a grocer and a printer also had premises here.

Farther along, Stamford House was built in 1720 and, like The Keir, has now been converted into flats. In its early days The Keir, built in 1789, was occupied by West Indies merchants and then by a prominent Roman Catholic family who built a chapel in the grounds. A late owner (1900) was Richardson Evans who founded the John Evelyn Society in 1903.

After passing the high defensive looking walls of the large private house at the turning into Camp Road, one may wonder about the age and origins of the variously-styled houses and cottages of the friendly looking row called West Place. Many of these date back to the eighteenth century and the land at their rear, now occupied by a group of well designed modern almshouses with access from Camp Road, is where the old workhouse (1750) used to stand.

Farther along Camp Road, past the old 'Fox and Grapes' and the modern almshouses, one may also wonder about the unusual octagonal building which now forms part of a new school for handicapped children. This is the Round School which began life in 1760 as a charity school for fifty children of "the deserving poor" and was in continuous use as a school until its closure in 1965. After that the building languished for many years under threat of demolition and only after a long battle waged by conservationists was the decision made to preserve it.

The Round School

After taking one westward past Camp Cottages (owned by the Royal Wimbledon Golf Club), and a few private houses, Camp Road marks the end of the conservation area. Beyond it lies the golf course, the open common and that mysterious earthwork, Caesar's Camp, whose fosses were ploughed out by a thwarted would-be developer a hundred years ago, before the Board of Conservators could take preventative action.

This therefore may be a good place to pause and reflect before turning back. Probably the most important key to Wimbledon's past has been lost for ever but, hopefully at least, a new age has dawned when such acts of social vandalism do not – or need not – happen anymore.

Appendix

List of Conservation Areas in Greater London

BARNET
    Barking Abbey Grounds and Town Quay 21.10.75
    Chipping Barnet, Wood Street 20.12.68
    Finchley, Moss Hall Crescent 8.10.74
    Hampstead Garden Suburb 20.12.68
    Mill Hill 20.12.68
    Monken Hadley 20.12.68
    Totteridge 20.12.68

BEXLEY
    Bexleyheath, Red House Lane 7.3.74
    Old Bexley 12.2.71

BRENT
    Roe Green Village 22.11.68

BROMLEY
    Anerley, Belvedere Road 22.3.73
    Beckenham, Chancery Lane 17.5.73
    Chelsfield 4.2.72
    Chislehurst 4.2.72
    Orpington, St Paul's Cray 16.5.74

CAMDEN
    Belsize 7.12.73
    Bloomsbury 2.1.69, 27.7.73 and 19.10.73*
    Camden Square 1.11.74
    Charlotte Street 3.5.74
    Covent Garden 30.3.72*
    Elsworthy 7.12.73
    Eton Villas 7.12.73

Hampstead Village 9.5.68, 19.12.68 and 27.11.70*
Highgate Village 17.5.68*
Kelly Street 1.8.75
Parkhill Road 23.2.73 and 13.4.73
Primrose Hill 18.2.72
Regent's Canal 10.5.74
Regent's Park 25.7.69

CORPORATION OF LONDON
Amen Court 16.4.71
Bank 16.4.71
Bow Lane 16.4.71
College Street 16.4.71
Finsbury Circus 16.4.71
Fleet Street South 16.4.71
St Andrew's Hill 16.4.71
St Bartholomew's 16.4.71

CROYDON
Addington Village 17.8.73
Coulsdon, Bradmore Green 24.5.68
Croydon:
    Parish Church 19.11.71
    The Waldrons 11.5.73
Upper Norwood:
    Church Road 15.3.74
    Harold Road 18.5.73
Webb Estate 2.11.73

EALING
Bedford Park 22.7.69
Brentham Garden Estate 22.7.69
Ealing Green 22.7.69
Hanger Hill Garden Estate 22.7.69
Hanwell, Churchfields 22.7.69, Village Green 16.7.75
Northolt Village Green 22.7.69
Norwood Green 22.7.69

ENFIELD
Edmonton, Church Street 28.8.70
Enfield Town 25.10.68 and 27.7.73
Forty Hill 1.11.68
Ponders End, Flour Mills 28.8.70
Southgate Green 11.4.68
Trent Park 14.6.74

Turkey Street 27.7.73
Winchmore Hill:
  The Green 1.11.68
  Vicars Moor Lane 28.8.70

GREENWICH
Blackheath 1.3.68*
Charlton Village 3.9.71
Deptford Albury Street and St Paul's 16.10.75
Eltham Green 11.7.75
Eltham Palace 3.9.71
Eltham Progress Estate 3.9.71
Greenwich Park 22.5.70*
West Greenwich 1.3.68*
Woolwich Common 11.7.75

HACKNEY
Albion Square 28.11.75
Arlington Avenue 4.7.69
Clapton:
  Clapton Common 31.1.69
  Clapton Pond 31.1.69
  Clapton Square 31.1.69
Clissold Park 31.1.69
De Beauvoir Town 7.1.72

HAMMERSMITH
Fulham:
  Bishop's Park 8.7.71
  Hurlingham 8.7.71
Hammersmith:
  Brook Green 8.7.71 and 26.4.74
  Imperial Square 27.8.75
  St Peter's Square 8.7.71
  The Mall 8.7.71
  Parson's Green 22.8.75
  Queen's Club Gardens 22.8.75
Ravenscourt Park and Starch Green 26.4.74
Shidindge Street/Acfold Road 22.8.75
Walham Grove 22.8.75

HARINGEY
Crouch End Crescent Road 25.10.74
Fortis Green 1.3.74
Highgate 17.5.68

Muswell Hill 1.3.74
North Tottenham 12.1.73

HARROW
Harrow on the Hill:
    Harrow Park 29.8.69
    Roxeth 29.8.69
    School 18.10.68*
    Sudbury Hill 29.8.69
    Village 18.10.68*
Pinner:
    High Street 5.7.68*
    Tooke's Green 21.1.71
Stanmore, Little Common 20.8.70
    Old Church Lane 21.11.75
    Stenmore Hill 21.11.75

HAVERING
Cranham 4.3.69
Gidea Park 3.7.70
Havering-atte-Bower 15.5.70
Rainham 4.3.69
Romford, Central Area 22.11.68

HILLINGDON
Black Jack's Lock 31.7.75
Coppermill Lock 31.7.75
Cowley Lock 27.3.75
Denham Lock 3.7.75
Eastcote 15.3.73
Harefield 30.1.70
Harmondsworth 30.1.70
Hillingdon Hill/Village 15.3.73
Ickenham 30.1.70
Old Hayes 30.1.70
Ruislip 15.3.73
Springwell Lock 31.7.75
Uxbridge, The Greenway 16.10.75
Uxbridge, Windsor Street 19.7.73
West Drayton Green 15.3.73

HOUNSLOW
Bedfont Green 7.4.75
Bedford Park 30.4.70
Isleworth Riverside 14.12.71

Old Chiswick 5.6.69
Strand-on-the-Green 23.1.69
The Butts 13.2.69

ISLINGTON
Arlington Square 4.7.69
Barnsbury 27.11.69
Canonbury 20.11.69
Charterhouse Square 22.8.69
Clerkenwell Green 11.4.69
Cross Street 4.9.70
Duncan Terrace/Colebroke Row 4.7.69
Highbury Fields 4.7.69
Highbury New Park 4.4.75
Keystone Crescent 4.9.70
Newington Green 4.9.70
New River 11.4.69
St Luke's 4.4.75
St Mary Magdalene Church Gardens 22.8.69
Tufnell Park 4.9.70
Whitehall Park 22.8.69 and 19.4.73

KENSINGTON & CHELSEA
Aubrey House 30.6.72
Brompton Square 30.6.72
Campden 30.6.72 and 14.5.73
Carlyle Square 30.6.72
Chelsea New Church (St Luke) 30.6.72
Cheyne 15.7.69 and 18.12.73
De Vere 19.12.69 and 13.2.73
Earls Court Square 21.11.75
Earls Court Village 26.6.73
Elm Park 30.6.72
Edwardes Square and Scarsdale 6.3.70
Hans Town 30.6.72
Holland Park 30.6.72 and 5.1.73
Kensington Palace 30.6.72
Kensington Square 14.2.69
Kensington Village 6.3.70
Ladbroke Estate 14.2.69
Markham 30.6.72
Milner Street 30.6.72
Norland Estate 14.2.69*
Pembridge Estate 14.2.69

Phillimore Estate 30.6.72
Queens Gate 19.12.69 and 30.6.72
Royal Hospital 15.7.69 and 30.6.72
Sloane Stanley (Gertrude Street) 19.12.69
Smith's Charity & Thurloe Estates 15.8.68
St Quintins/Oxford Gardens 11.7.75
The Boltons 6.3.70, 30.6.72, 26.6.73 and 14.8.73

KINGSTON UPON THAMES
Kingston Old Town 30.4.71
Old Malden:
    Manor House/Hogsmill River 30.4.71
    Plough Green/Church Road 30.4.71
Surbiton, St Andrew's Square 30.4.71

LAMBETH
Albert Square 15.8.68
Brixton Road 15.8.68
Brixton Water Lane 2.1.70
Clapham 15.8.68
Garrads Road 2.1.70
Gipsy Hill 2.5.75
Hackford Road 10.5.74
Hanover Gardens 13.5.69
Kennington 15.8.68
Lambeth Palace 15.8.68*
Lansdowne Gardens 15.8.68
Northbourne Road-Clapham Park Road 16.5.75
Rectory Grove 15.8.68
Stockwell Park 15.8.68 and 29.2.72
Sunnyhill Road 20.7.73
Vassall Road 15.8.68
Walcot Square 15.8.68

LEWISHAM
Blackheath 25.7.68 and 26.11.70*
Brockley 11.10.73
Brookmill Road 15.2.73
Deptford, Albury Street and St Paul's 16.10.75
Halifax Street 15.2.73
Jews Walk/Kirkdale 11.10.73
Lee Manor 1.8.75
Mercia Grove 1.8.75
Perry Fields 1.8.75

St Stephen's Church 15.2.73
Stanstead Grove 22.5.75
Somerset Gardens 15.2.73
Sydenham Park 15.2.73

MERTON
Merton Park 6.9.68 and 30.7.71
Mitcham, Cricket Green 18.7.69
Wimbledon Village 6.9.68

NEWHAM
Three Mills 11.11.71 and 8.10.71

REDBRIDGE
Snaresbrook 29.10.70
South Woodford 29.10.70
Wanstead Park and Village 29.10.70
Woodford Bridge 29.10.70
Woodford Green 29.10.70
Woodford Wells 29.10.70

RICHMOND UPON THAMES
Barnes:
    Barnes Common 7.2.69
    Barnes Green 7.2.69
East Sheen:
    Percy Lodge/Christchurch Road 7.2.69
    Thorne Passage 7.2.69
Ham Common 7.2.69
Ham House 28.11.75
Hampton Court and Village 7.2.69
Hampton Wick 5.12.69
Kew:
    Kew Green 7.2.69
    Lawn Crescent 6.12.74
    Lichfield Road 7.2.69
Petersham 7.2.69
Richmond:
    Central Area 7.2.69
    Richmond Green 7.2.69*
Richmond Hill 7.2.69*
    Riverside 7.2.69*
Teddington:
    Park Road 28.2.75

Twickenham:
  Cambridge Park/St Stephens Gardens 6.12.74
  Riverside 7.2.69*
  St Margarets Estate 10.12.71
  Trafalgar Road 7.2.69
  Twickenham Green 7.2.69

SOUTHWARK
  Addington Square 9.7.71
  Bermondsey Street 9.3.73
  Borough High Street 27.9.68
  Camberwell Grove 17.7.70
  Camberwell New Road 27.9.68
  Caroline Gardens 27.9.68
  Dulwich Village 27.9.68 and 5.11.71*
  Glengall Road 23.5.74
  Holly Grove 9.5.75
  Kennington Park Road 27.9.68
  St Mary's Rotherhithe 9.10.70
  St Saviours Dock 29.3.74
  Sceaux Gardens 27.9.68 and 11.4.74
  Trinity Church Square 27.9.68
  West Square 17.9.71

SUTTON
  Beddington 30.7.70 and 17.5.74
  Carshalton Village 21.5.68
  Cheam Village 19.2.70
  Wrythe Green 16.12.69

TOWER HAMLETS
  Albert Gardens/Arbour Square 9.9.69
  Artillery Passage 28.9.73
  Bethnal Green Gardens 9.9.69
  Elder Street 9.9.69
  Fashion Street 9.9.69
  Island Gardens 19.3.71
  St Anne's Church 9.9.69
  St George's Town Hall 9.9.69*
  Stepney Green 9.2.73
  Three Mills 11.11.71 and 8.10.71
  Tomlins Grove 9.9.69
  Tredegar Square 19.3.71
  Wapping Pier Head 9.9.69
  York Square 9.2.73

WALTHAM FOREST
Browning Road 29.3.74
Forest School 5.1.73
Walthamstow, St Mary's Church 13.12.68
Woodford Green 17.3.72

WANDSWORTH
Charlwood Road 12.2.70
Clapham Common 25.3.69
Coalecroft Road 12.2.71
Lifford Street 28.7.70
Nightingale Lane 13.10.70
Old Battersea 9.11.72
Parkfields 19.8.69
Putney Embankment 1.4.71
Roehampton Village 29.7.69

WESTMINSTER
Bayswater 4.4.68
Belgravia 4.4.68
Birdcage Walk 8.5.70
Charlotte Street West 31.10.74
Covent Garden 30.3.72
Dorset Square 30.5.68
Government Precinct 3.7.70
Grosvenor Gardens 3.7.70
Harley Street 16.1.69
Knightsbridge 4.4.68
Maida Vale 4.4.68 and 6.10.72
Mayfair 18.9.69, 14.12.73 and 11.4.74*
Millbank 22.1.70
Molyneux 14.12.73
Pimlico 28.11.68 and 14.12.73
Portman Estate 4.4.68*
Regent's Park 18.9.69
Regent Street 14.12.73
St James's 18.9.69
St John's Wood 4.4.68
Strand 31.10.74
Soho 18.9.69
Stratford Place 16.1.69 and 6.10.72
Westbourne 14.12.73
Westminster Cathedral 28.11.68*

Bibliography

The Civic Amenities Act and Town and Country Planning Acts
Civic Trust Index of Conservation Areas
Policies for Conservation Areas (Civic Trust)
Local History Collections (London Borough Libraries)
Official Guides of the London Boroughs
GLC List of Scheduled Buildings and Information Sheets
Publications by various Conservation and Amenity Societies
Guides to the Parish Churches
Survey of London, various volumes (The Athlone Press) 1973
Handbook to the Environs of London by James Thorne 1876, (new
    edition by Adams & Dart 1970)
A City at Risk by Simon Jenkins (Hutchinson) 1970
Nairn's London by Ian Nairn (Penguin) 1966
Nicholson's Guide to the Thames (David & Charles)
Crossing London's River by John Pudney (John Dent) 1972
Middlesex by Bruce Stevenson (Batsford) 1972
A Dictionary of National Biography (Oxford)
Blackheath Conservation Area – An Initial Study (London Borough of
    Lewisham) 1969
Carshalton – From Medieval Manor to London Suburb by A.E. Jones
The Story of Dulwich (London Borough of Southwark Neighbourhood
    Histories No.2)
Wandering through Dulwich by George Brown (A 'Villager'
    production)
Dulwich, the Village of Edward Alleyn (A 'Villager' production)
Dulwich Village by D.H. Allport (Cardercraft Publishing Service)
    1937
An Account of the Urban District of Enfield by Cuthbert Wilfrid Whitaker
    (George Bell & Sons) 1911
Forty Hall, Enfield (London Borough of Enfield)
Capel Manor Institute of Horticulture (London Borough of Enfield
    Education Committee)

A History of Greenwich by Beryl Platts (David & Charles) 1973

The Streets of Hampstead, compiled by Christopher Wade (High Hill Press in association with the Camden History Society) 1972

The Heathside Book of Hampstead and Highgate, edited by Ian Norrie (High Hill Books) 1962

Bygone Hanwell by Montagu Sharpe (Brentford Publishing & Printing Company)

A History of Greater Ealing by Cyril M. Neaves 1931 (reprinted by S.R. Publishers 1971)

Hanwell Village Green, Report of Studies (London Borough of Ealing) 1974

Harrow through the ages by Walter W. Druett 1956 (reprinted by S.R. Publishers 1971)

Harrow Walkabout by Elizabeth Cooper (Pinner & Hatch End W.E.A.) 1973

The History and Antiquities of Highgate by Frederick Prickett, 1842 (reprinted by S.R. Publishers 1971)

Holland House in Kensington by Derek Hudson (Peter Davies) 1967

Holland Park (A GLC Publication)

Old Kew, Chiswick and Kensington by Lloyd Sanders (Methuen) 1910

Kingston-upon-Thames, A Dictionary of Local History by G.B. Greenwood (Martin & Greenwood Publications)

Old Kingston by George William Ayliffe (Knapp Drewett & Sons) 1914

History and Heroes of Old Merton by Kathleen Denbigh (Charles Skilton) 1975

Northolt Village Green, Report of Studies (London Borough of Ealing) 1973

Pinner through the Ages by William W. Druett (The Hillingdon Press) 1937

Pinner in the Vale by Edwin M. Ware 1955

A Pocket Guide to Pinner (The Pinner Association) 1972

Richmond by Kathleen Courlander (Batsford) 1953

A Prospect of Richmond by Janet Dunbar (Harrap) 1966

Wimbledon has a History by Guy Boas, C.S. Cloake & H.J. Warren (The John Evelyn Society) 1947

History of Wimbledon by R.J. Milward

Cannizaro House, Wimbledon and its Park by William Myson and G.J. Berry (The John Evelyn Society) 1972

Index